# The Topless plays

# The Topless plays
## Miles Tredinnick

Three one-act stage plays
for solo performance

Topless in London
Topless in Philadelphia
Topless in Sydney

Topless in London, Topless in Philadelphia, Topless in Sydney.

All rights whatsoever in these plays are strictly reserved and application for professional or amateur performance should be made before rehearsal to the author Miles Tredinnick.
email: *MilesTredinnick@aol.com*

**Topless in London** (originally published as Topless)
Copyright ©1999 & © 2006 by Miles Tredinnick

**Topless in Philadelphia**
Copyright © 2009 & © 2014 by Miles Tredinnick

**Topless in Sydney**
Copyright © 2014 by Miles Tredinnick

ISBN-13: 978-1505449495
ISBN-10: 1505449499

This edition printed by CreateSpace 2015

Cover illustration by Brendan Murphy.

# The Topless plays

Introduction – Going Topless

# Miles Tredinnick

Miles Tredinnick's comedy stage plays include *Twist, Topless, Laugh? I Nearly Went to Miami!*, *Up Pompeii*, *Topless in Sydney*, *It's Now or Never!* and *Topless in Philadelphia*. For BBC1 TV he created and wrote the comedy series *Wyatt's Watchdogs* and was also a writer on the show *Birds of a Feather*. In addition, Miles wrote stage and television material for Frankie Howerd, including the Channel 4 special *Superfrank* and the stage comedy *Up Pompeii*. His first novel was *Fripp*. He is the lead singer Riff Regan in the British rock band *London*.

For more information: *www.MilesTredinnick.com*

# Introduction – Going Topless

One of the best jobs I've ever had was working for The Big Bus Company as a London tour guide on their open-top buses. The Big Bus specialised in the very best tours around the capital and still does today.

As might be expected summer is the busiest period of the year in sightseeing and time-off a rare beast. Somehow, however, I had managed to get myself a few days off. It was a hot weekend in early July so I decided to escape the stifling city heat and drive down to Devon.

On the Saturday, after a relaxed evening at a Babbacombe pub I slipped off the kerbstone landing in a broken heap in the gutter. The pain was agonising and I didn't need the doctor at the nearby Torbay Hospital to confirm what I already knew - I had broken my ankle.

Back in London, it was obvious that I wasn't going to be able to tour guide for a while. This presented me with a problem. What was I going to do with all that spare time?

Robert Goodman, my friend and colleague at Big Bus (and the man who had trained me as a guide) suggested that I should write about something I knew about.

One thing I did know inside-out was being a London tour guide. After all I had been doing it five days a week for the previous four years. I rested my plastered leg up on a stool, switched on my PC and started tapping away. Before long I had a first draft of a comedy stage play called *Topless*.

I constructed the play as an actual tour of London. The stage set would be an open-top deck of a sightseeing bus and the tour guide would be Sandie, a bubbly Londoner, with problems.

I decided to make her story a domestic tale, something that everyone could identify with. And why not make it simple? She would be madly in love with her husband Duncan, a photo-lab technician, who does the dirty on her by having an affair with his female assistant.

And we get to hear all about it because nearly every-thing on Sandie's tour of London seems to remind her of something to do with her straying husband.

My intention was to make the play light and fun when the tour begins and then make it slowly slide into a dark, sinister ending with Sandie revealing how she may or may not have murdered her husband as revenge for his philandering. The latter being revealed as her bus drove past the atmospheric Tower of London.

It was like *Shirley Valentine* meets *On the Buses*. Only with a Hitchcock edge.

The play written, my next job was to find a director to bring it to life. Martin Bailey was also a tour guide for the Big Bus Company but he had trained as an actor and was keen to get into directing. I sent him a copy of *Topless* to read. Twenty-four hours later he called me up to tell me he loved the play and wanted to direct it.

Over the next few weeks, we started making plans for an early autumn production. We began looking for a suitable venue. We must have checked out every fringe theatre in London but we couldn't afford even the cheapest rent. It was hopeless.

Despondent, one afternoon Martin and I met up in a bar off Shaftesbury Avenue and over a few beers decided to axe the whole idea. Maybe it was just beyond our capabilities and budget.

It was then that Martin suggested "Why don't we do it on the bus itself? Perform the play for real so that when Sandie points out Piccadilly Circus on your right, there it is for real on your right."

It was total virtual reality and a brilliant idea.

The next day Robert Goodman got us a meeting with Richard and Eleanor Maybury, the owners of The Big Bus Company, and we pitched the 'play on a bus' idea. Always receptive to any new thinking they were immediately enthusiastic and an opening night was pencilled in for September. We would run the show six nights a week. They would supply the bus and a driver every night and all Martin and I had to do was produce the play on the top-deck!

We put an advertisement in *The Stage* and held auditions on the upper deck of an open-top bus down at the Big Bus depot in Earlsfield, south-west London.

Actress after actress came up the stairwell, plugged in the microphone and gave an audition piece. There were plenty of good 'Sandies' that rainy afternoon but the outstanding one was Rachael Carter.

Rachael was an exceptionally talented performer who came originally from Blackpool. She had a superb sense of comedy timing and a lovely twinkle in her eye. Just what we were looking for.

We offered her the part of Sandie and she accepted it.

Rehearsals got underway and as it was too expensive to do them on a real tour bus driving around London, Martin would drive a hire car along the route with Rachael pointing out the sights from the passenger seat. Sometimes I sat behind her with a script and acted as prompter. It was probably the first time an entire play had been rehearsed in a Hertz rental saloon!

Richard and Eleanor Maybury, true to their word, started scheduling a theatre bus to leave from beside The Ritz Hotel in Piccadilly every night at 7.30.

Their brother Desmond had a special open-top Big Bus painted with a huge poster of *Topless* on its side. This was a stroke of genius and typical of Des. All day long whilst the bus was running around London picking up tourists for Big Bus sightseeing tours, it was giving our little play massive publicity. And as TV news crews are always filming in the streets of London (how many times have you seen a reporter standing in front of The Houses of Parliament?) we were getting the name of the play on national TV many times a day.

Brendan Murphy, a Sales Controller at Big Bus turned out to be a fantastic artist and came up with a stunning poster for us. It was great to see it displayed all over London.

Interest from the press was high too. Our publicity girl Sara Tauxe did a great job getting us on the BBC news and countless foreign TV programmes who couldn't believe that these mad English people were performing a play on a bus.

The first night came up and was a resounding success. Rachael Carter's performance was a triumph managing to pull off the bubbly side to Sandie's character equally as well as her darker side.

The end of the play where she explains how she would commit the perfect murder, in the shadow of The Tower of London, worked a treat. Just like I had always hoped it would.

I loved seeing *Topless* go out night after night packed with theatregoers who were willing to try a different kind of theatrical event.

One night I 'rode the show' as we called it and when the play had finished got into conversation with a middle-aged American and his wife from Texas.

Out of curiosity I asked him what he had thought of the evening. He replied "Really enjoyed it but that tour guide should really concentrate on the sightseeing. All she went on about was her damn husband Duncan! Who cares about him? We wanted to hear about the sights. Someone should have a word with her and tell her to leave her problems at home."

It turned out that he and his wife had really believed that they were on a genuine sightseeing tour. They had no idea that it had been a play when they bought their tickets!

A higher compliment would have been impossible to get.

These days the *Topless* plays are usually found being performed inside theatres, village halls and pubs but I have heard of the odd occasion when some enterprising production company have ventured for the genuine article - on top of a real open-top bus.

I just hope it doesn't rain!

*Miles Tredinnick*
*London.*

# Topless in London
## Miles Tredinnick

Your tour guide is Sandie.

The action of the play takes place on the open-top deck of a London sightseeing bus on a summer's day.

Time: The present.

# Topless in London

*The front end of an open-top London sightseeing bus showing the wind-screen, the two front rows of seats and the top of the stairwell. There is a bus bell button on the top of the stairwell. The play can be staged in one of two ways; you can either use back-projection photos/videos/film of the London sights or simply let* **SANDIE**'s *words paint the pictures unaided. It is entirely up to your imagination.*

*When the lights come up,* **SANDIE** *is coming up the stairs, carrying a holdall bag, which she puts down on the floor. She takes her microphone out of it and plugs it in. She then addresses her tourists, (the audience).*

**SANDIE** *is a Londoner of indeterminate age. She's neatly dressed in blazer and skirt and very bubbly. She wears a photo ID card pinned to her lapel. She's very likeable and has an infectious giggle.*

*She reads from a clipboard in dreadful cod-French.*

**SANDIE:**
Bienvenue a Londres et Bienvenue chez 'London Topless Buses'. Le 'Topless' est le moyen ideal de visiter sans effort les sites touristques de Londres. Je m'appelle Sandie et notre chauffeur est Sid... *(She realises something is wrong and shouts down the stairwell.)* Sid? Are you sure this is the group from Calais? Because they don't seem particularly French to me... They've what?... Cancelled? Oh... Well thanks

for telling me. *(Facing audience.)* So you all speak English do you? Well I won't be needing that. *(She puts the clipboard down on one of the front seats.)* Hi everyone and welcome to London.

My name's Sandie and I'm your tour guide. How are you all? Everyone OK? I'm feeling absolutely brilliant today. I am. Honestly. Now I know what you're thinking. The wheel's turning but the hamster's dead. But don't worry, I haven't got going yet. I'm building up to my tour de force and believe me it'll be worth waiting for.

We're going to have a fabulous tour. Now 'cos I thought you were all going to be foreign I've brought along a few *visual aids* to jazz things up a bit. *(She opens her bag and throws out various soft toy London souvenirs into the audience starting with a miniature Big Ben.)* This is Big Ben which we'll be seeing later. Who wants Big Ben? *(She then takes out a little Beefeater doll.)* And here's one of the Yeoman Warders you'll see down the Tower. *(Next she produces a policeman's helmet and throws it to a man.)* Evening all! *(She salutes him and bends her legs.)* Love your helmet sir. Smashing. *(She holds up a large plastic cigar.)* And what's this one? It's Winston Churchill ain't it. *(She throws it to someone.)* You hold that and wave it when I get to me Churchill bit. *(She then holds up something wrapped in silver foil.)* And what have we got 'ere? Oh me sandwiches. Only cheese and tomato I'm afraid. If anyone wants to do a swop later I'm game. Provided it's not meat. I'm a veggie.

Right, that's the basics dealt with so off we go. (*She presses the bus bell button twice. We hear the ding-ding.*) Now our driver is called Sid, he's the best driver in the country. Hopeless in town but in the country he's brilliant!

*The bus starts up. It jerks off.* **SANDIE** *grabs a safety rail to steady herself. From now to the end of the play street noises can be heard where appropriate.*

See what I mean!! Hold on tight! Right, now I'm going to take you on a fabulous trip around London. I'm going to show you all the big sights. Trafalgar Square, Big Ben, The London Eye, St Paul's Cathedral, all the way down to the Tower of London. So sit back and enjoy yourselves. If you've got any questions keep them to yourselves! I haven't got time for questions; I'll be too busy talking! I'm the original motor-mouth, me.

Now we're kicking off in Piccadilly Circus...
*(Brightly coloured lights in background.)*

Where are all the elephants I hear you asking? And the clowns? Where are the clowns? Well there aren't any. The word 'circus' is a Latin word. It means round-about or circle. Behind the electric signs is Soho. Oh yes? I see a few of you men smiling at the mere mention of the name. It's a night place ladies. You know, clubs and stuff. I used to be a stripper once you know. I did. I'm not ashamed of it. I used to work in this dump called *Madame Bridget's Hot Bodies A Go-*

*Go Club*. I was a topless table dancer. I was. I only did it for the money. I was a bit desperate I have to admit. I'd been signing on for twelve months and then I saw this ad in the paper for dancers and went along. Had to jack it in though. I used to get giddy standing on the tabletops in me high heels, to say nothing of the sparks I got off the pole! So I left and the next job I got was this. So I'm still topless but this way I'm out in the open air. T'riffic!

Over on your right there is the statue Londoners call Eros, *the Greek God of lurve*. They say that if you stand underneath it on the stroke of midnight and declare your love to your beloved, that love will last a lifetime. Aaah. I'm not sure that's true. I met my husband Duncan under there one night and my goodness have we had our share of problems. Still you don't want to hear about my troubles with Duncan do you? Of course you don't, you're all here to see the sights.

On the left is Shaftesbury Avenue, that's where all the theatres are. Actually the first time I met Duncan wasn't under Eros, it was on this bus. Not that he was actually *on* the bus, he sort of ran *into* it. On his motor-bike. Made a big dent at the front. It was over there on the corner of Regent Street wasn't it Sid? My good-ness, what a carry-on that was. Duncan claimed it was Sid's fault but we won't go into that. Anyway I got talking to Duncan and I found I really liked him. He was gorgeous. *The spitting image of Mel Gibson.* He had long hair and the most beautiful green eyes. And

he was all leathered up. I like a man in leather. Of
course he didn't sound like Mel Gibson 'cos he came
from Manchester. Spoke *like that*. You know like the
*Oasis* boys. And of course he was half Chinese on his
mother's side. So if you can imagine a leathered up,
half Chinese long haired Mel Gibson lookalike who
sounded *like that*, well that was Duncan. He was
gorgeous. Anyway he…

Oh, straight ahead of you is Leicester Square. That's
where all the movie premieres are held. Do you know
what Duncan told me he did when I first met him? He
said he worked in films so I thought hello, hello bit of
glamour here, know what I mean girls? Turned out not
to be films as in movies as in Hollywood but films as
in snapshots as in Cricklewood. He worked in one of
those places where you dropped your holiday pics in
and come back an hour later and discovered what a
crap photographer you were. Anyone remember them?
Long before we all had cameras on our phones. It was
called *Well Developed*.

*Cut brightly coloured lights.*

We're now in the Haymarket. Back in the seventeenth
century this is where you brought your horses and
gave them hay and stables and things whenever you
came to London. Anyway, where was I? Oh yes.
Duncan, he asked me out. We tried to blag our way
into *Stringfellows* by telling the bouncer Duncan was
Mel Gibson. Didn't work though. Turned out the

bouncer hated Mel Gibson. Thought he looked like a girl. Honestly! Some people…

Ah, now on your left is Orange Street. That's where the street walkers used to ply their trade back in the old days. It was a whores' paradise. They'd do anything for a shiny sixpence. Up with the crinoline down with the knickers…

**AS VICTORIAN WHORE:** *(East End accent.)* Wot's your fancy sir? Oooh! That'll cost you an extra shiny sixpence if you want me to do *that.*

It was a huge red light district. If you want a laugh look at that road sign. *(She points.)* "*Humps for 100 yards*".

On your right is the musical *The Phantom of the Opera.* I haven't actually seen it myself. It's always sold out. I've heard it's quite good. All about this beautiful girl with a great aria who falls in love with some weird looking musical genius. Andrew Lloyd Webber. He wrote it didn't he? He writes all the shows.

On the right is a street called Pall Mall. Named after King Charles II's balls. He used to get people to whack 'em. With mallets. All the knobs would stand in a line and whack away. It was a sort of Italian game a bit like croquet. Very popular I believe. Pall Mall was one of the first streets to be lit with gas lamps. Probably so they could have a few night matches.

Anyway to cut a long story short I saw Duncan off and
on for about three weeks. Trouble was when I was off
he was on. Some slag called Carol. She worked at
HMV in Oxford Street and got him half-price CDs. I
only found out about her by accident. Whenever I
went round his, there were CD boxes all over the
place. I knew he was up to something. For one thing
he didn't have a CD player. And for another I found
her soaking in the bathtub. Bitch. So we had a big row
as you'd imagine and I told him it was over but he
called me later and said he was sorry and would I at
least meet him for a drink. So like a fool I agreed. We
arranged to meet under Eros, *the Greek God of lurve,*
and of course he said he was sorry and I said I'd forgive him and we kissed and hugged and it was all
lovey-dovey. Flippin' hell, if I knew then what I know
now I would've pushed him into the bleedin' traffic!

National Gallery on the left, loads of paintings. We're
now in Trafalgar Square. Laid out to commemorate the
Battle of Trafalgar in 1805. That was a naval battle
between the British and the combined forces of France
and Spain. Won by us under that man on top of his
column, Horatio, Lord Nelson. Admiral of the Fleet.

On the other side is the South African High
Commission, South Africa House. See the golden
springbok leaping out on the corner of the building?
Doesn't it look beautiful? Up there on the balcony was
where President Nelson Mandela waved to thousands
of people in the square a few years ago. Did you see it
on TV? It was brill. I was here. And on that day, and

that day only, we had two Nelsons in Trafalgar Square. Not as many pigeons as there used to be. In the old days it was the only place in London where you could feed the birds and have a pigeon sit on your head. And that's sit. Spelt S.I.T.

*Fade-up the sound of horses' hooves clip-clopping along Whitehall.*

Oh look, quick! There's the Household Cavalry on their way to Horse Guards' Parade. Don't they look handsome? The Queen's Life Guard. They're not supposed to talk to you. In fact if you ask them a question you won't get an answer. Some ladies tuck their phone numbers into the men's boots hoping to get a phone call later when they're off duty. I did that once when I was about seventeen. I wrote something like "Hi. My name's Sandie and I'd love to go out with you" followed by my phone-number. Nothing happened for five weeks and then I got a call from some old cobbler who was re-heeling the boot. He was very disappointed. He thought Sandie was the name of one of the Horse Guards.

*Fade-out the horses' hooves.*

Can you see those big black gates ahead of you on the right? They guard the most famous address in this country. Number 10 Downing Street. That's where the Prime Minister works. I'm not really into politics. Just a load of men in suits having affairs with their secretaries. (*This strikes some sort of chord. She*

*pauses.)* Duncan looks good in a suit. When he bothers
to wear one. If we're going out somewhere special.
Like a wedding. I love a wedding don't you? Everybody dressed up with somewhere to go. It was at a
wedding that Duncan proposed to me. It was my
brother Tim who was getting hitched. He's in corp-
orate catering and he fell in love with Nikki who
butters the sandwiches. (Nikki spells her name with
2Ks by the way; she's a bit particular. Tends to look
down on other Nickies that spell theirs with one K or
the more traditional CK). Anyway, it was a great day.
Duncan was Best Man. He had to make a speech of
course. God it was funny. He stood up and clinked a
fork against a glass to get some quiet and guess what?
The glass smashed. Bits went flying everywhere.
Some of it landed in the bride's grandfather's ice-
cream sundae. He didn't notice though. Just carried on
eating. He thought it was bits from the nut brittle
topping. It was only when his tongue started bleeding
that he knew something was up. Laugh? We never
stopped. You had to be there really…

*Fade up the sound of Big Ben chiming four o'clock.*

We're now coming into Parliament Square, the
political centre of London. Who's got Big Ben?

Hold it up then, wave it round. There's the real thing
on your left. Big Ben's not the name of the clock; it's
the name of the enormous bell inside the tower.
Weighs thirteen and a half tons. Named after Sir

Benjamin Hall. Good job his name wasn't Sir Richard Hall. Eh?

Right who's got the Churchill cigar? The Houses of Parliament is where Winston Churchill had that famous run in with Bessie Braddock. Has anyone heard that one? (*She uses a plastic cigar to impersonate Churchill.*) What happened was Winston Churchill came back from lunch one afternoon slightly, you know, intoxicated. Sounds discourteous to say he was drunk so let's just say he was merry, all right? In fact he was as merry as a newt. Probably had one too many of the old brandies down his club. Anyway he bumps into this Bessie Braddock who can't stand the sight of him. She smells his breath and in a very loud voice so everyone can hear she shouts out "Winston Churchill. You are drunk. DRUNK!" And he turns around looks her right in the eye and says "Mrs Braddock. You are ugly. UGLY! But in the morning I shall be sober." Oh he was one with the one-liners that Churchill. If he'd been around today he probably wouldn't have gone into politics. More than likely he'd have been writing gags for some TV sitcom. He would. He could knock 'em out. I'll give you another example of his quick-fire-wit. It happened between Churchill and Lady Nancy Astor. She was an American from Virginia and the first female Member of Parliament to take her seat in the House. Anyway, one afternoon all the MPs were in there, you know, debating and what-have-you, when Lady Astor lost her rag at some remark Churchill had made. She stood up shaking her fist and said "Mr Churchill you're an absolute disgrace, if you were

married to me I'd poison your coffee!" Winston
Churchill slowly rose to his feet and said "Lady Astor,
if I was your husband, I'd drink it". Oh that Churchill.
He had more one-liners than Del Boy. There's a statue
of him on your right. The old bulldog.

Anyway, where was I? Speeches, wedding, tongues,
blood, oh yeah, Duncan, that's right. We were in this
hotel having a slow dance at the reception. I think the
DJ was playing *Lady in Red* you know by Chris de
Burgh. I love that song. And I was the lady in red. I
was wearing my satin red dress and cream shoes from
Christian Lacroix. I knew I looked good. In fact let's
not mince words here, I looked *stunning.* I was ze
knees of ze bee. Anyway, Duncan held me close and
whispered in my ear. He said:

*AS DUNCAN: (Manchester accent.)* Sand, how about
you and me doing it?

And I said:

*AS HERSELF:* What? Here? In front of all these
people?

And he said:

*AS DUNCAN:* No, get hitched. Tie the knot.

It was very romantic. He was a bit pissed of course.
He'd had quite a bit to drink to get up confidence to
make his Best Man speech. But I could tell he meant

it. That he loved me. And of course I loved him. So I said *YES*!!! It was the happiest moment of my life up until then. I felt brilliant inside ... then the music changed. I think it was Frankie Goes to Hollywood and *Two Tribes.* And he started dancing like men do when they're pissed. *(She imitates Duncan wildly dancing.)* And he fell over. Landed on Nikki-with-2Ks left thigh. The one with the blue garter on it.

We're now on Westminster Bridge crossing the river Thames. That's the real reason why London is here. Almost two thousand years ago the Romans came to the banks of the river Thames after they invaded this country in AD 43. They didn't know where the hell they were going, a bit like you lot really, but where they built a bridge over the river, they called the surrounding city Londinium. And this became London. Londinium isn't a Latin word in itself so we're not really sure where it came from. Of course I've got my own little theory about the name. Do you want to hear it? Yeah? All right then. Well I reckon there were probably already some people living here when the Romans arrived. Peasants I expect, just sitting around with their chickens and sheep and going about doing peasanty things. And the leader of the Romans probably went up to one of them and said 'What's this place called mate?' And the peasant probably grunted back "*Londinium*!". Which was probably an old word meaning "*Sod off you bastards!*"

Anyway, where was I? Weddings, garters, proposals, Frankie Goes to Hollywood, oh yeah, Duncan. He

asked me to marry him. My dad had a fit. My mum
was all right, I think she fancied him herself. She
always had a thing about a certain Australian actor.

**AS HER MUM:** *(Warm London accent.)* He's very
sexy love. Looks just like Mel Gibson in *What Woman
Want* but sounds like Johnny Depp.

But my dad ...well he never liked Duncan. When I
first took him home dad hardly said a word to him. He
said he didn't like his manner.

**AS HER DAD:** *(Strong Scottish accent.)* I don't like
him Sandra. Looks like Mel Gibson in *Mad bloody
Max* but sounds like Johnny Vegas.

Which was a strange reaction considering Mel's
brilliant portrayal of William Wallace in *Braveheart.*
But this woman wanted Duncan, so dad got overruled.

We got married in a registry office and it was the
happiest day of my life. It was like walking down the
aisle with you-know-who. Although there wasn't
actually an aisle, it was more of a corridor – they had
the builders in the main room – some kerfuffle with
the ceiling. I wanted to get married in a church, you
know the full white wedding, but Duncan insisted on a
registry office. Said he wasn't religious. So we got
married in a civil ceremony in Cricklewood. It was all
right though. But his mother... Oh don't talk to me
about his mother. Don't start me off on her... Silly
cow. Face like a raw turnip. We've never got on. Oh

no. She never saw me as a good match for her precious
Duncan. Never thought I'd make a good wife.

*AS DUNCAN'S MUM: (Strong accent.)* You not
good for him Sandcastle...
*AS HERSELF:* SANDIE!
*AS DUNCAN'S MUM:* You not good for him. He
special boy. You go away, leave him alone. OK with
you?

*(With a smug grin.)* If I knew then what I know now...

St Thomas' Hospital on the right. A special place for
me 'cos it's where I was born. Honest. My mum had
come up to town to see Engelbert Humperdinck at the
Royal Albert Hall and went into labour in the back
row of the stalls. Apparently her waters broke during
the second verse of *Please Release Me.* The ambul-
ance got here just in time. There's a museum here
dedicated to our greatest nurse Florence Nightingale,
the Lady with the Lamp. As opposed to me mum who
was the lady with the lump.

Just behind St Thomas' is Lambeth Palace, the official
London home to the Archbishop of Canterbury. And
beside that is St Mary-at-Lambeth Church. That's
where Captain Bligh of *Mutiny on the Bounty* fame is
buried. I love those Bounty films don't you? Which
one's your favourite? Clark Gable? Marlon Brando?
Mine's the one with Mel Gibson in it. Whenever I see
it I imagine my Duncan strutting about on the poop

deck polishing his telescope. *(As Captain Bligh.)* "Mr Christian, this is mutiny!"

On the left is the old GLC building. The Greater London Council as was. Now it's all hotels and luxury apartments. In the bottom of it is the London Aquarium. Which is great if you're into fish. Duncan would often drag me in there. He's potty about tropical fish. Has all sorts. Rare ones too. Red Fire-fish, Blue-spotted-longfins, Spiny puffers. I don't know, they were all in our flat swimming about in this huge tank behind the telly. I used to think it was quite sophisticated really, like something out of *Dr No*. Fish are Duncan's biggest love. He buys them from this bloke in Milton Keynes who imports the rarest species from abroad. We would often drive down there on his Triumph and on the way back I would sit pillion behind him clutching these plastic bags of water containing these fish. Once, one of the bags burst and a Madeira Rockfish got stranded in the middle lane of the M25. My God! Duncan went mental. We stood helpless on the hard shoulder and watched as an *Ikea* van squashed the bugger flat. Still those fish used to make him happy. And if he was happy, I was happy. So there we all were. Him, me and the fish.

(*SANDIE points up to her right*.) Now do have a look at that ladies and gentlemen. The *London Eye*, one of the tallest observation wheels in the world. 135 metres high. Impressive isn't it? You step into one of those glass pods and up you go. Brilliant views. Have you heard about the latest craze to get married on it? It's true. Apparently you have to get married when you're right at the top. The highest point. Nothing else will do. You only have a few minutes to exchange your vows. Then like most marriages, it's downhill all the way…

*She removes her blazer and puts it down on one of the front seats.*

That's better. It's very sticky today isn't it? Mind you, we had good weather for our honeymoon, Duncan and I. Only rained one day in two weeks. We went to the Canaries. Tenerife. Duncan took lots of photos which he later developed himself in his shop. Just as well as some of them were a bit, well, racy. If they'd gone through Boots we'd probably have been arrested. It was really nice though. Just the three of us. Oh I didn't tell you did I? His mother came too. Cow. Didn't have any choice really. She paid for the trip. Got it at discount on account of her working part-time in a travel agent.

*AS DUNCAN'S MUM:* I give you nice present in Canary place, Sandbag...
*AS HERSELF:* SANDIE!
*AS DUNCAN'S MUM:* I give you nice present but cheaper deal for three than two. So I come too. OK with you?

*She shakes her head at her mother-in-law's insensitivity then suddenly spots someone in the street.*

Oh look! There's that actor wot's-his-name. You know the one on the telly in that soap. You know who I mean. The one with the pudding basin haircut who's always being told about his bad breath. Thingy. Wot's-his-name? *(She waves.)* Cooee! Hello. *(She abruptly stops.) My God he gave me the finger!!* Maybe it's not him. Looks like him though. Dead ringer. You never know who you might spot as you go round London. You want to keep your eyes open. I once saw a breakfast television weather girl. I did. Can't remember her name now but she was the one who stood in front of the map with her huge boobs. Her left tit always blocked out Cornwall.

So when we got back from our honeymoon Duncan and me moved into his little flat in Cricklewood. It was above his shop actually. He did some sort of deal with the landlord. It was all right except for the smell of developer. God that got up my nose. Terrible pong. Anyway, the flat was a bit small but we liked it. And of course Duncan didn't have far to go to work. Just down the stairs really so he could have a bit of a lie-in every morning, and more often than not a bit of the old morning glory...

*AS DUNCAN:* Not getting up just yet are you Sand?

Ah, we're now crossing Waterloo Bridge. The longest bridge in central London. This bridge is where we can see the two cities that make up London. On the left is the City of Westminster, a thousand years old and on the right is the City of London almost two thousand

years old and originally built by the Romans. It's
amazin' innit? Sid, slow down so they can take some
photos…

*She takes a gulp from a plastic water bottle.*

Anyway, after the wedding we moved into the little
flat above *Well Developed.* I'd keep it nice and clean.
You'd never have found any dust in there. Spotless. I
was really happy. I didn't miss going out to clubs and
stuff. I mean, after we'd finished at *Madame Bridget's,*
me and the girls would often go out clubbing. Have a
bit of a laugh. But what's it all about? You spend your
life going out to meet men don't you? It's a game.
Single women going out trying to meet single men and
vice-versa. Trying to find Mr Right. Or *Mr Right
Now!!* It's always been like that. And when you find
what you think is the ideal bloke, you fall in love and
marry him, if you're lucky. And then you settle down.
And that's what we did. In Cricklewood above *Well
Developed.*

On your right is Somerset House better known as the
former offices of the General Register of Births,
Deaths and Marriages. The hatch 'em, match 'em and
dispatch 'em place. Anyway, we were really happy in
our little flat. Apart from one thing. It was about this
time that we discovered we couldn't have kids… You
can imagine the pressure from his mother.

***AS DUNCAN'S MUM:*** Why no kids, Sandpaper? My
boy make good father. Get on with it. OK with you?

*AS HERSELF:* No it's not OK with me. Or him.
Mind your own business, turnip face!

We're now approaching Covent Garden. There used to
be a fruit, veg and flower market here once. Have you
seen *My Fair Lady*? This was where Professor Henry
Higgins first met Eliza Doolittle. I used to love that
film when I was small. I would pretend I was Audrey
Hepburn and my little brother Timmy would be Rex
Harrison. I nearly choked once. Timmy kept trying to
make me talk proper by filling me mouth with gob-
stoppers. Silly really. Timmy didn't look anything like
Rex Harrison. He'd stand there in his short trousers
making me say 'The rain in Spain stays mainly in the
plain' again and again. But I loved Rex Harrison. He
was one of my first crushes. He was, honest. Him and
that odd looking bloke in *Boney M. (She considers
this.)* God, no wonder I turned out like I did.

The thing was Duncan and I really wanted kids. We
really did. So we went for it hammer and tongs so to
speak but nothing happened. I said we should both go
and have tests and see what could be done. Duncan
didn't want to do that though. I think he thought it was
unmanly or something, going into a cubicle with a
porn-mag and a jam-jar. So I secretly went and had my
own tests and eventually discovered it was me who
couldn't. God that came as a shock I can tell you.
Some blockage somewhere. I never told Duncan, I just
kept it to myself. I wish I had done now. I still did a bit
of this, the tour guiding, in the summer anyway. Looking back it was probably the worst decision I made.

You see back then before mobile phones, people tended to take loads more pictures in the summer so Duncan was working twelve, fourteen hours a day developing and printing. It was all getting a bit much so he decided to do something. One day he said to me:

*AS DUNCAN:* I'm taking on an assistant, Sand.

And that's when *she* came into our life.

On the left is the London School of Economics. That's where Mick Jagger was a student but he left early 'cos he couldn't get no satisfaction.

Anyway, where was I? Oh yeah. Sonya Grey. She wasn't even very pretty. Long black hair and pinched features. I called her the *Hawk*. She had that sort of look as if she was about to swoop down from a height and claw a sheep. But that aside she seemed OK. She just came in at nine-thirty in the morning and stood behind the counter all day taking in people's rolls of film and working the till. Apparently she'd done something similar working in Wednesbury.

*AS THE HAWK: (Flat, vacant Black Country accent.)* If you want an extra set of prints we have a special 2 for 1 offer on. Quite a saving, I think you'll find.

Duncan was out the back in the dark room doing the real work. At least that's what I thought. But there's other things you can get up to in the dark of a dark room. Things started developing, if you know what I

mean, between Duncan and the *Hawk* and I'm not
talking Kodak paper here. I came back from work
early one afternoon and could hear him and her in
there. Heavy breathing and stuff. But you know it's
very difficult if two people are at it in a dark room.
You know they're in there but they have the perfect
excuse for not unlocking the door.

***AS DUNCAN:*** Just a few minutes love, there's a film
developing. Be out in a moment.

It's hopeless. By the time you get in there it's all a red
glow and everybody's peering at strips of negatives.

The *Hawk* tended to avoid the darkroom after that but
I knew something was going on. You just know don't
you?

(*Points to her left.*) Now here's a lovely little church.
St Clement Danes, the central church of the Royal Air
Force. The bells ring out the nursery rhyme "*Oranges
and Lemons*". Do you know that one? I do. My nan
used to sing it to me when I was small. It's like a
conversation between all the bells of all the London
churches. Do you want to hear a bit of it? All right
then. I'll see if I can remember it…

(*She sings.*) "Oranges and lemons,
Say the bells of St Clement's.
Pancake and fritters,
Say the bells of St Peter's.
Two sticks and an apple,

Say the bells at Whitechapel.
You owe me five farthings,
Say the bells at St Martin's.
When will you pay me?
Say the bells at Old Bailey.
When I grow rich,
Say the bells at Shoreditch.
Pray, when will that be?
Say the bells at Stepney.
I'm sure I don't know,
Says the great bell at Bow.
Here comes a candle to light you to bed,
Here comes a chopper to chop off your head."

*A beat. She immediately turns to her right.*

Royal Courts of Justice on the left. The second highest
civil court in the land. Civil litigation only. Suing
someone or getting a divorce.

*She pauses, reflecting on what she's said.*

Anyway, so what was I to do? I was convinced
Duncan was having an affair with the *Hawk* so I
decided to turn detective. I reckon he'd got wind that I
suspected something. Him and the *Hawk* didn't go in
the dark room so much. In fact some days she didn't
go in there at all. So where were they liaising?
Because liaising they were. I was convinced of that.
He was meeting her somewhere. Most evenings he
was out till quite late saying he was meeting business
acquaintances. But I knew he was seeing her. I mean

there were only so many *Well Developed* franchise
holders around. He said I could always get hold of him
in an emergency by texting him. Frustrating things
texts aren't they? Occasionally I would leave a mess-
age like *(She mimes tapping a text.)* "Where R U and
wot R U doing?" Talk about being naïve. As if he'd
text me back and say "Shagging. Nearly finished. B
home soon. Duncan." But I knew where he was anyway. You didn't have to be Inspector Morse to work
that one out. There was only one place he could be.
Round hers.

*She turns and looks ahead.*

That's Monument to Temple Bar and it's very
significant. As soon as we pass it we enter the City of
London. It's not very large, the City. About one square
mile big.

So I decided to stake out the *Hawk's* place in Kilburn.
Wasn't very grand. She lived in this grotty one bed-
roomed ground floor flat. It did have a little garden out
the back though. All overgrown of course. Anyway,
there was a tree about halfway down, perfect cover. I
climbed over the wall at the back and set up position
and on the very first night I saw them...

*We hear a street newspaper vendor shouting
"Standard! Standard! Get it here."*

Oh, hold the front page! We're going down Fleet
Street. For over 300 years this is where we published

our newspapers. Not many papers here today though, they've all moved out. But some great writers started along this street. Arthur Conan Doyle, Charles Dickens, Jackie Collins. They all wrote for newspapers and magazines. Still there's one legacy left over from the journalistic days. The pubs! Fleet Street's a great place for a pub-crawl. There are more pubs along this street than almost anywhere else in London. Now there's a sobering thought...

So where was I? Grotty flat in Kilburn, stakeout, oh yeah, Duncan. I was watching the two of them in her kitchen. She was struggling to get the cork out of a bottle of wine. She just couldn't get it out so she passed it to Duncan. He was pulling and pulling with the bottle stuck between his legs. His face was getting redder and redder. *(She mimes this.)* And then it happened. His back went. He's always had a bad back. The slightest thing sets it off. You should see him, doubled-up like a Himalayan Sherpa. Well there was a real drama then. She was running around trying to help him and he kept saying…

*AS DUNCAN:* Don't touch me, don't touch me.
*AS THE HAWK:* What's the matter Dunky?
*AS DUNCAN:* Me back's gone…
*AS THE HAWK:* Lie on the bed, I'll rub it.
*AS DUNCAN:* NO!

It was a right fandango. I thought there's no point in me staying so I went home and knocked back half a bottle of vodka. I tried to imagine what I was going to say when Duncan came in. Shouldn't have bothered really. By the time he got back, all doubled up, from the *Hawk* I'd passed out on the sofa. I woke up in the morning with this cracking headache and there he was lying beside me on the floor fixing his back. He has to remain rigid for a minimum of three hours on the parquet. I didn't say anything that morning. About him and the *Hawk*. I hadn't actually seen anything. Not really. No, I had to get hard evidence.

Well it didn't take me long. Two weeks later I was busy doing me ironing when Duncan comes up from the shop and says he wants to talk to me. Something important he says.

*AS DUNCAN:* Could I have a word, Sand?
*AS HERSELF:* Of course, Dunc.

Well, he only went and told me straight out he'd been sleeping with the *Hawk*. No hesitancy, no nothing.

*AS DUNCAN:* I think you should know that I've been seeing Sonya. We've been having a... er relationship.
*AS HERSELF:* Oh…

That really knocked me sideways. I mean I know I already knew but for him just to tell me matter of factly like that, well, it cut through me like a knife. It really hurt inside. But nothing he said could prepare me for what was coming up. He then told me she was pregnant and was going to have his baby.

By this time I didn't know where to look, my eyes were all over the place. I was looking in every direction but his. It was the bombshell from hell. I was speechless. Well as speechless as you can be when you're throwing an iron at someone.

Mind you I didn't hit him. I don't know whether it was me eyes not looking at him or what but the bloody iron ended up in his flamin' aquarium! The top was off because earlier I'd been feeding them. There was this huge flash and all the fish got electrocuted. They were all floating on top of the water. He went berserk! Never mind him and the *Hawk*. He just went into one saying I'd deliberately murdered his precious Blue spotted-friggin'-longfin-wotsits!

*AS DUNCAN:* You bloody woman!! I'll never build a collection like that again!

He went mental! Well by this time I'd turned on the waterworks. I was bawling and all that and he seemed to calm down a bit. So we tried to have a frank discussion about him and the *Hawk*. Didn't resolve anything. She was three months gone, he claimed he was in love with her and that night he moved out. As simple as that. Packed a suitcase and walked out. I felt so alone that night. Just me in that bloody flat. Me and a tankful of fish all floating on the surface and staring at me with dead eyes.

*She turns and looks ahead.*

There's St Paul's Cathedral. Wren's masterpiece.
We'll be up there in a minute. Tell you more then.
Anyway, it always amazes me how quickly one
recovers from something if you've got a goal. And I
had a goal all right. I wanted Duncan back whether the
*Hawk* was pregnant or not. I've been dumped too
many times to realise that if you don't get in there
straight away you lose ground. Strike while the iron's
hot.

I had my opportunity because Duncan was still opening up the shop every day although he was actually
living with *her*. By this time of course the *Hawk*
wasn't working with him. I'd have throttled her if
she'd taken one step over the threshold and she knew
that. So I made it my business to go down and see him,
bring him a cup of tea occasionally and that sort of
thing. I think I threw him to be honest with you. Hell
hath no fury and all that and there was I dropping
down to see him every ten minutes like Mary flippin'
Poppins.

The Old Bailey's on the left. Our Central Criminal
Court. See the statue of Justice on top of the dome? I
wonder what it's like to stand in the dock in there? At
least they don't hang people anymore. Ruth Ellis was
the last woman to be hanged in this country. July 13,
1955. She murdered someone for love. It's not as
uncommon as you might think ...

So there I was declaring my undying loyalty to the rat
and to be honest I did still love him. I really did. Even

after all he'd done I was still in love with him. And
then there was an extraordinary turn of events…

*Fade-up a peel of church bells.*

St Paul's Cathedral. Took Christopher Wren thirty-five
years to build and was opened in 1710 in the reign of
Queen Anne. Of course we all remember St Paul's
from 1981 don't we? This was where Prince Charles
married Diana.

*Fade-out the bells.*

So where was I? Oh yeah, it was a Wednesday and I
went down to see Duncan, took him a cup of tea. He
was busy in the dark room but he said he wouldn't
mind if I joined him. In fact he said he'd like the
company. It was weird being in there in the dark with
him. Just the red glow. Almost romantic in a funny
sort of way. As he developed pictures of other
people's holidays we started talking about this and that
and to be honest we were getting on better than we had
in months. He didn't mention the *Hawk*. I don't know
whether it was deliberate or not. In fact I had to bring
her into the conversation. I said something subtle like
…

***AS HERSELF:*** How are you getting on with wots-
her-face?

And to my astonishment he said they'd been having filthy great rows, he'd been banned from the bedroom and was having to sleep in her front room.

*AS DUNCAN:* She's got me kipping on the sofa, Sand. With my back!

Well you could've knocked me down with a throw-away camera. I said what was the problem and he told me that he reckoned she had faked the pregnancy because now she claimed she had miscarried and he didn't believe her. Well... I couldn't believe what I was hearing. It sounded too good to be true, if you know what I mean. The *Hawk* and him hardly talking and she not expecting any more. Talk about a turn-around. Anyway, you can guess what happened can't you? Yeah, that's right. It just felt right. Him and me thrashing about on the floor underneath the enlarger and fixing tanks. It was fantastic. Until afterwards. He got a text. From her. Don't ask me what it said but it must've been something lovey-dovey because the next thing he's pulling on his jeans and getting ready to go. I said:

*AS HERSELF:* Where are you going then?

And he said:

*AS DUNCAN:* Back to hers.

So I said:

*AS HERSELF:* But I thought you were having terrible rows and kipping on the sofa hurting your back and all that.

And he said:

*AS DUNCAN:* I'm sorry, I can't help myself. I love her and I want to be with her.

And off he went. Just like that. The bastard. I felt used, cheated, crippled inside… It was at that precise moment that I knew I was going to have to cause him some serious grief. My head was exploding with it all…

BRING OUT YOUR DEAD! BRING OUT YOUR DEAD! That's what they were shouting in these very streets in the long, hot summer of 1665. The year of the Great Plague. The bubonic plague. The flea living on the rat spread it. They reckon about one hundred thousand died in all. A third of the population of London. It was appalling. Men walked up and down these streets shouting out "Bring out your dead" so they could cart the corpses off to the plague pits. There was a terrible stench of rotting flesh 'cos they couldn't get 'em out fast enough. Mothers taught their children to sing a little rhyme as they played on the streets hoping it would ward off the fever. Some of you probably know it.

*(She sings.)* "Ring, a ring o'roses
A pocketful of posies.

A-tishoo! A-tishoo!
We all fall down."

Anyone heard that? Let me tell you what it meant.
'Ring, a ring o'roses' was when you knew you'd
caught the plague. You had a thumping hot temp-
erature and a rash of rosy, red rings all over your body.
'A pocketful of posies' were the herbs and spices
you'd have about your person to ward off the fever.
Remember there was no medicine in those days. No
antibiotics, nothing. 'A-tishoo! A-tishoo!' was when
you started sneezing. Continuous sneezing was the
final symptom. Once you started sneezing you knew
you were going to die. 'We all fall down.' Well that
was when you snuffed it. A terrible way to go.

On the left is St Mary-le-Bow church. Famous for its
Bow Bells. They say that if you're born within the
sound of Bow Bells you can call yourself a London
Cockney.

Anyway where was I? Diseases, plague, rats. Oh yeah,
Duncan. How was I going to get my own back? Punish
him. Because that's what I had to do and let me tell
you it's not that straightforward. Oh no...

My first idea was to kill him. I know, I know, you
probably think I'm completely mad. Alfreda
Hitchcock. Well I probably was. I was so wound up
inside. I didn't even think of any consequences.
Duncan had hurt me beyond repair so the obvious
solution was to get rid of him, permanently, so he

could never, ever do it again. So, accept, that was my
state of mind. Not normal I know but I'm sure all of
you at some time have harboured similar thoughts.
Anyway it was a pointless exercise. Even if you do
want to kill your old man where do you find someone
to do it? I mean you hardly go on Google and put in
'Contract Killers', do you?

*She mimes making a phone call.*

**AS HERSELF:** Hello? Is that Contract Killers-r-us?
**AS LONDON THUG:** That's right. Want someone
taken out?
**AS HERSELF:** Well I'm not sure. How do you
actually do it?
**AS LONDON THUG:** You leave that with us little
lady. We're the experts.
**AS HERSELF:** How much does it cost?
**AS LONDON THUG:** 25 grand.
**AS HERSELF:** Oh. Do you take Visa?

Oh hang about, I nearly forgot. The Great Fire.
London had just got over the plague when the
following September there was another disaster. The
Great Fire of 1666. Started in Thomas Farriner's
baker's shop over there in Pudding Lane. (*Points to
her right.*) One night one of his ovens caught fire and
to his horror it set alight the roof made of thatch. That
ignited the building beside it, which in turn burnt
down the next building and so on. Within four days
and five nights, four-fifths of London had burnt down.
But, you know, sometimes two wrongs do make a

right. 'Cos the fire wiped out the plague. Some say it destroyed the rats.

We're now on London Bridge.

*(She sings.)* "London Bridge is falling down,
Falling down, falling down.
London Bridge is falling down.
My fair lady".

Oh, this is where they used to put the heads of executed prisoners. *(Pointing above her head.)* They'd stick 'em on the end of a pikestaff at the entrance to the bridge as a sort of warning to others. Hang on, I've got one of me visual aids somewhere. *(She dives into her bag and pulls out a transparent polythene bag containing the head of a man with long hair, blue facial war-paint and a ferocious stare. It is incredibly lifelike.)* The first ever head put up was William Wallace the Scottish patriot. Remember the movie *Braveheart*? Wooh!! He looks a bit angry doesn't he? *(She holds the head up to eye-level and stares at it.)* Hmm… reminds me of someone…

*She puts the head down on a seat.*

Anyway, I couldn't get someone to kill Duncan but I had to get at him somehow…

Oh by the way, just down here beside London Bridge is where the 'Nancy Steps' were. As in Charles Dickens's novel *Oliver Twist*. This is where Nancy

betrayed Bill Sikes and he murdered her. Do you
remember that? I do.

*She stares down over the side of the bus for a beat and
then continues.*

It was over the next few weeks that things started
becoming clearer in my mind. I thought I'd try another
angle. Don't do anything at all. Lay off Duncan. Give
him a bit of space. I figured it wouldn't take too long
for him to get bored with the *Hawk* and then he'd
come back to me. And I'd forgive him and we'd start
again and put all this dreadful business behind us. We
might even adopt a baby. I liked that idea. I did. That
we could be a little family and all that. In fact it gave
me a certain piece of mind. It kept me going through
that dark period when everything was topsy-turvy.

My doctor put me on tranks which helped of course.
To a certain extent anyway though now I'm not so
sure that those pills didn't affect my mental judgement
a bit. So there I was sort of floating along in limbo
land waiting for Duncan to get bored with the *Hawk*
when one day something awful happened. Have you
ever had one of those days? When you think it just
can't get any worse and then it does. That's what
happened to me. I remember it so well.

I'd been down Tesco's and had just stumbled back
with me groceries when I saw a letter on the hall floor.
It was from some solicitors informing me that Duncan
was seeking a divorce. On some grounds or other. I

couldn't take it in to be honest; I was that much
shaking with anger. I immediately went downstairs to
the shop to have it out with Duncan.

*AS HERSELF: (Waving an imaginary letter.)* What's
the meaning of this?

*AS DUNCAN:* I'm sorry if I've hurt you Sand but the
fact is I'm in love with Sonya and I want to marry her.
That's all there is to it.

Well, I lost it I'm afraid. I went mad. Swore at him and
called him every name under the sun. I was appalling.
Everything came out. Dark-rooms, fish tanks, turnip-
faced mothers, you name it. Anyway there was no
changing his mind. He wanted me out of the flat and
out of his life. ASAP.

I just couldn't accept it. I didn't know what to do next.
I knew I had to do something but what? This time I
really did feel like killing him but that would've been
too easy. Now I wanted revenge. I wanted Duncan to
suffer for all the hell he had put me through. But killing him wasn't the answer. If I really wanted to cause
him grief I had to hurt him in the strongest way
possible. Make him really suffer. And in order to do
that I'd have to kill *her*! The *Hawk*. And if I could do
that … Well it just felt the right thing to do. And
although I know I would never have been capable of
killing Duncan, however much I now hated him, I was
confident I was capable of killing *that cow.*

I think it was on a Thursday afternoon when I realised that the perfect time to kill the *Hawk* would be the last Saturday of the month. Why? Because that particular Saturday was Duncan's birthday. What better day to kill her than on his birthday? That way he would be constantly reminded of her every year. Now all I had to do was come up with a foolproof method of murdering her.

I spent every day deep in research. I read anything that would provide me with a method of killing. I went to the library and took out Agatha Christies, Ruth Rendells, even old Sherlock Holmes stories. I did. But nothing was as inspirational as *The London Dungeon*. London's horror museum. It shows you all the terrible things that have happened to London over the centuries. The fire, the plague, the rats, the torture, the blood, the gore, the horror, the fear, the terror... You name it, it's in the Dungeon. It's like Madame Tussaud's Chamber of Horrors times ten!! It was mind provoking. Especially the Jack the Ripper stuff. You see, like him, I was after the perfect murder. One that could be suitably carried out without the slightest lead coming back to me.

In three weeks I became an authority on murder. I learnt how to poison, I learnt how to cause accidental death, I learnt how to kill in every manner possible. And not get caught. It's amazing you know. If you want to become a killer, there are more books to tell you how to do it than if you wanted to save life and train as a doctor.

I became an authority on death. But strangely enough
it was none of the methods I read about that became
my final choice although I'm not saying that they
didn't spark me off. My choice of the way I was going
to kill the *Hawk* was all mine. It was totally my invention. And it was foolproof. It had to be. It had to be the
perfect murder. One that even Columbo wouldn't be
able to solve…

*Distant heavy thunderclouds can be heard. From now
to the end of the play it gets gradually more overcast.*

Oh dear, rain's on its way. What a shame. Anyway,
this was my plan, right? I'd get up as normal on the
day, do a bit of housework, usual stuff. I'd then pop
downstairs to the shop and say hello to Duncan.

*AS HERSELF:* Hello Duncan.
*AS DUNCAN:* Oh… er hi.

No doubt he'd be too busy to talk which would be fine
by me. I'd probably wish him happy birthday though.
I'd then ask him if I could borrow his little van to do
some shopping. He'd be bound to say yes just to get
me out of there. I'd then drive to where the *Hawk*
lived, slip on a wig, sunglasses and a bit of lippy, go
up to her front door and press her buzzer. She'd be
surprised to see me of course, after all we hadn't
spoken for months. Chances are she wouldn't
recognise me straight away so I'd explain the wig was
a new look I was trying out. She'd probably make a

few derogatory remarks saying it didn't suit me or something…

***AS THE HAWK:*** Don't mean to be funny but that colour doesn't really suit you.

… as if she'd know anything about style, then before she could ask me why I'd called round I'd tell her that I'd come to terms with Duncan leaving me and setting up with her and now just needed to clear the air with her. She wouldn't want me in there, that's for sure, but I'd just push past her anyway and go straight into her lounge.

Now I knew this next bit would upset me. I'd have to steel meself. Many of Duncan's things would be in that room. I've envisaged it so many times in my mind. His books. A framed photo of him and her on the mantelpiece perhaps. One of his jackets slung on the back of a chair the way he always used to do… It would all be so bloody cosy. But of course running alongside the wall would be his beloved aquarium.

*THAT BLOODY FISH TANK MEANT EVERYTHING TO DUNCAN.* The day he came back for it and took it out of our flat was the day that I knew he wasn't coming back. Ever. But little did anyone know that glass receptacle was going to provide me with my method of killing her. To give the *Hawk* her due I'd imagine she'd try and accommodate my visit. She'd offer me a drink…

*AS THE HAWK:* Fancy a cuppa?

… and I'd say yes although I knew I wouldn't be
drinking it. I wouldn't even touch the cup. No way. I
wouldn't want anything to incriminate me. Nothing
should show that I was ever in that flat.

So whilst she'd be dithering about in her kitchen, I'd
slip on a pair of Marigolds that I'd have in my bag, nip
over to the aquarium and open the top. I can imagine
all the little fish immediately coming up to the surface
with their little mouths opening and closing. Chances
are she'd have forgotten to feed them…

*AS THE HAWK:* I'm always forgetting to feed his
fish.

I'd then take a plastic bag out and rip it open. A torrent
of water would flood out into the tank. There'd be a
vibrant flash of colour, velvety orange-brown and blue
stripes would slip under the surface. I'd then look
around for something to drop in there. Could be anything. An ornament off the mantelpiece, a paper-
weight, a flowerpot, it doesn't matter. As long as it
sunk to the bottom of the tank. I'd then close the lid on
the aquarium, take my rubber gloves off and sit down.

*Another clap of thunder.*

The *Hawk* would then come in with her tray of tea
things and join me. She'd probably start making small

talk, chat away about something that in her pea-sized brain was important…

*AS THE HAWK:* Did you see *EastEnders* last night?

… and then I'd suddenly look over to the aquarium with an innocent puzzled look and ask her why the object was in there under the water? The look on her face would be a picture.

*AS THE HAWK:* What's that doing in there? That shouldn't be in there.

She wouldn't be able to understand it at all. There'd be total bewilderment. Her one brain cell would be on time-and-a-half. She'd go over to the tank. I'd follow her. She'd open the top and plunge her hand into the water to get the object out. And then it'd happen… *She'd scream with the pain.*

*A huge clap of thunder.*

The tailfins of the Indian Ocean Clown surgeonfish exude a horrible poison. Just like I read in one of Duncan's fish books that he'd accidentally left behind in the flat. Very painful. So whilst she was running around in agony I'd pick up the nearest heavy object (maybe the teapot?) and bring it down on her head. Klunk!! She'd be out cold. Simple. The *Hawk* would be lying there on the carpet. But I wouldn't gloat. Oh no. Too much to do.

I'd wrap her up in some bin-liners, drag her outside and dump her in the back of the van. Oh hold on a tick, here comes the Tower of London. I'll tell you the rest in a minute. Better put your brollies up as we cross Tower Bridge though. Here it comes…

*Heavy rain starts to fall. She opens up an umbrella.*

Ever since William the Conqueror built the original Tower with his brother around 1078, this castle has been associated with imprisonment, torture and execution. Seven people have had their heads cut off here including Anne Boleyn and Catherine Howard, two of King Henry VIII's six wives. They'd be led onto the executioner's block and PHEWW!!! - it was all over. In one cut of the axe if they were lucky.

*More thunder.*

So where was I? Oh yes, I've bungled the *Hawk* into the back of the van. Nobody sees me do it. I'd then drive down to an isolated part of the Thames that I know, remove her clothes and throw her into the water. It'd be that easy. It really would. The body would go off with the current and that'd be the end of it. Until later of course. The police would be bound to find the body at some stage and fish it out. Duncan would have reported her missing and presumably he'd be asked to go and see if he could identify her. But of course he wouldn't be able to. Because just before I threw her in the river *I cut her head off!*

*She quickly pulls out a transparent polythene bag containing a woman's head with long black hair. It is grotesque.*

Oh no, this isn't her. This is Anne Boleyn. One of me *visual aids*. Ugly old cow, isn't she?

*She puts the head back in the bag and zips it up.*

A brilliant plan, wouldn't you agree ladies and gentlemen? Unfortunately I never found out whether it would have worked or not because something extraordinary happened…

When I arrived at her flat, all dolled up in my wig and what-have-you, the Hawk was coming out with loads of suitcases and piling them into the back of a taxi. Despite my cunning disguise, she recognised me straight away…

*AS THE HAWK:* Oh hello, what are you doing here?

She told me that she'd found out that Duncan was having an affair with some trollop called Tina.

*AS THE HAWK:* He's shagging the cow. She owns the Dollis Hill franchise for *Well Developed.*

Well. Would you believe it? The *Hawk* apparently had had enough and was off to live with her sister in Sutton Coldfield. She'd known about the affair for a while but had decided to move out today as it was his birthday. I thought great minds think alike. She then said the landlord wanted the flat vacant ASAP so he could move in some Russian students. Would I mind asking Duncan to pick up his fish tank?

Would I mind? I said I'd be delighted.

*A pause.*

Trouble is Duncan's disappeared. No one's seen or heard of him for weeks. He's completely vanished. God knows where he is. If you see him, tell him to get in touch. You can't miss him; he's the spitting image of Mel Gibson.

Well, that's the end of my tour folks. Welcome to London…

*She unplugs her microphone and carrying her holdall, starts to walk down the stairs. She suddenly remembers something and reappears.*

Silly old me, I forgot me head…

***SANDIE*** *picks up the William Wallace/Mel Gibson head from the seat and exits.*

*Blackout.*

# Topless in Philadelphia
## Miles Tredinnick

Your tour guide is Gus.

The action of the play takes place on the open-top deck of a Philadelphia sightseeing bus on a summer's day.

Time: The present.

# Topless in Philadelphia

*The front end of an open-top Philadelphia sightseeing
bus showing the windshield, the two front rows of
seats and the top of the stairwell. There is a bus bell
button on the top of the stairwell. The play can be
staged in one of two ways; you can either use back-
projection photos/videos/film of the Philly sights or
simply let* **GUS***'s words paint the pictures unaided. It
is entirely up to your imagination.*

*As the lights come up all we can see of* **GUS** *are his
legs and feet as he lies on his back fiddling with the
underneath of one of the seats. We can hear him,
however, as he is cheerfully whistling away as he gets
on with his work. His trusty tools of screwdriver,
wrench and hammer are resting on the seat itself.
Every now and then a hand appears, searches for the
right tool and takes it under the seat to be used. There
is a lot of banging and tapping.*

*Satisfied,* **GUS** *slides out from under the seat and is
admiring his work when he spots his busload of
tourists (the audience). He gets to his feet, picks up the
microphone and speaks to us. He wears a bright short-
sleeve shirt, a snazzy vest and a tie displaying a TV
cartoon character.*

**GUS** *is in his 40s. A jolly man, born and bred in
Philadelphia. He has a tendency to nasally 'snort'
with laughter when he's enjoying himself. It can come
at any time and is something that he is hardly aware*

*of. On the floor beside him sits a bag containing his
tools.*

**GUS:**
Hi, sorry about that. I was down there fiddling with
something. *(A big Philly style greeting.)* HOW YA'
DOIN? *(He checks the time, an old-fashioned watch
on a chain.)* We'll be moving along shortly folks, a
minute or two at the most. By the way, the name's
Gus. Gus Clover. I'm your tour guide on this open-top
bus. I know it's hot but we're totally air-conditioned
up here. *(Snorts with laughter.)* We call this 'going
topless' so let's just hope it doesn't rain!

I'm going to take you on a great tour of Philadelphia,
the City of Brotherly Love. We're going to see it all,
the Liberty Bell, the very building where they signed
the Declaration of Independence, Betsy Ross's house,
Benjamin Franklin's grave… He's one of my personal
heroes you know, Ben Franklin. Great inventor. He
invented the lightening rod… he did! Bet that shocked
you. *(Snorts with laughter.)* And bifocals. What would
we do without them, huh? Means you can watch your
TV and change your remote without having to switch
glasses.

I'm an inventor when I'm not doing this. Oh yes.
That's what I was doing under the seat. I'm working
on a tilt mechanism that allows the passenger's seat to
tilt backwards so they can look up at the high build-
ings or monuments. Like the William Penn statue
which we'll be seeing later. There he stands, our city's

founder at 548 feet high and my tilting seat lets you
see him in all his glory. Now I know what you're
thinking. I'm ahead of you. We inventors have to be.
Anticipation is the name of the game.

The thing is… *(He's interrupted by a tourist's
question, unheard.)* Yes ma'am we'll be leaving in a
few minutes. *(He checks his pocket watch again.)* I
know you're eager to get going. We're all eager to get
going. You want to see Philly and I'm the man to
show you. But we've got to wait for our driver Elvis.
*(Another question, unheard.)* I don't know why he's
not here but I have my theories, I can tell you.
*(Another question, unheard.)* Well, there's a bar on
Market and 8 and Elvis likes to get himself in the
mood. A couple of beers and he's happy. *(Snorts with
laughter.)* No, I'm only kidding. He's crossed the
street to answer a call of nature. *(Las Vegas style.)*
"Elvis has left the bus…"

Anyway, where was I? Oh yes, my tilting seat for
seeing the full glory of sights. Now, I know what
you're thinking. I'm ahead of you. You're saying to
yourselves "Isn't that what the neck muscles already
do Gus? Do we really need a tilting seat to look up at
high objects? Surely neck muscles have got that one
figured out?" And to a certain extent I agree. Neck
muscles are nature's way of allowing us to tilt our
heads up or down. But you see you're not thinking
laterally. You're not thinking, like me, with an
inventor's mind. Thinking laterally is the number two
name of the game. Because my tilt seat isn't aimed at

ordinary people, it's aimed at tourists *who already have their head in a neck-brace.*

Think about it. *(A triumphant smile.)* People with their head in a neck-brace can't move their heads like you and me. They're restricted. They've got this lump of plaster stuck around their neck and movement, up or down, is limited. And that's why my tilt-seat would be great for them. Yes sir. If you want to be an inventor, you have to think laterally. I offered my idea to the company but they weren't really interested. But as I always say, their loss my millions. *(He leans on the seat, it collapses.)*

*GUS spots someone down on the sidewalk and waves.*

Here comes Elvis… Hi ya buddy… Ready when you are… *(He presses the bus bell twice. We hear the ding-ding of the bell.)*

*The bus starts up. It jerks off. GUS grabs a safety rail to steady himself. From now to the end of the play street noises can be heard where appropriate.*

Off we go then. Just a quick word on safety. Keep your arms, legs and heads inside the bus at all times. We don't want to lose bits of you as we go along. Use your head, don't lose your head! And look out for tree branches! *(He expertly ducks as an (unseen) tree branch sweeps over his head from behind.)* See what I mean?

There's so much I'm going to tell you. This city, Philadelphia, I love. I'm born and bred you know, South Philly. Great area, near the Italian market. If you get a chance get down there. Try Pat's for their cheese-steak sandwich. Tasty! Tell 'em Gus sent you, they might give you extra. They always do for me especially on my birthday. And guess what? Today is my birthday. That's right. 43 years old today. And I know what you're thinking, "Gus you don't look a day over 25." Well that's because I once invented a time machine! *(Snorts with laughter.)* No, no I'm just kidding. I haven't invented that one yet although I have been looking into it…

Anyway, let's hop into my imaginary time machine and go back to the year 1682 because that's when it all started round here. William Penn was the man who founded our city. He was given the land by King Charles II of England. Let me explain, Penn's father, Admiral William Penn spent a lot of his money help-ing the King reclaim his throne in the 1600s. When the Admiral kicked the bucket, the King still owed the debt to his son so he proposed a deal to William Penn junior that gave him a huge chunk of land in the New Land instead of money. A 45,000 square mile tract along the Delaware River. Penn accepted and left England in 1681 on board his ship the *Welcome*. And you'll never believe…

*A tourist's cell phone starts ringing. This irritates*
**GUS**.

Look, do you mind? Please switch all cell phones off folks. It's bad enough competing with traffic noise without someone babbling on his or her phone. Incidentally, did you know that the telephone first saw the light of day in Philadelphia? Yes sir. A Scottish elocution teacher from Boston called Alexander Graham Bell first demonstrated his new invention at the Centennial International Exhibition in Fairmount Park.

*GUS allows himself a smile. He prides himself on the fact that he can connect a Philly fact with whatever's thrown at him.*

Now, where was I? Oh yes. William Penn created the name 'Pennsylvania' from his family name 'Penn' and 'Sylvania' which means woodland. And do you know where 'Philadelphia' comes from? It's two Greek words that mean 'Brotherly Love'. That's why we are known as the City of Brotherly Love.

I admire our City's founder so much. He did something. He got off his butt and created something. Just like an inventor.

Interestingly, Penn spent only four of his seventy-four years actually in Pennsylvania... And when he died in England in 1718, he was penniless. Wasn't much brotherly love around when he croaked. Makes you wonder whether it was worth the trip? My wife Lynda always says why bother to see the world when you've got cable? Mind you, lately I've had quite a few problems with the brain of America …

Well, it was good in the beginning I'll say that. I met Lynda down at our public library. Not the most romantic place in the world I guess, with all those books blocking sight lines, but it was where she was working at the time. I was returning a book, I think it was one on advanced plumbing (I was going through a big home improvement phase at the time), anyway I saw this cute girl with long red hair standing behind the counter bar-coding some books and we started talking. I gave her what I thought was a bit of a Ben Franklin opening line…

*AS HIMSELF:* Books are like snowflakes, no two are exactly the same…

She looked at me like she didn't understand what I meant so I repeated myself and she mumbled something.

*AS LYNDA:* Mmm?…

It was a bit hard for me to hear actually as I had this cold and my ears were blocked up and you know how everyone whispers in those places. Anyway, we eventually started talking and I don't remember exactly how but the conversation somehow got around to the fact that her washing machine was broken and flooding her kitchen. She said…

*AS LYNDA: (Strong Southern accent)* There's this huge old puddle all over my tiles. I just don't know what to do.

She was originally from South Carolina incidentally, so I said...

*AS HIMSELF:* Why don't I come over and fix it? I'm great with washing machines. Yes ma'am!

And she looked at me, thought about it and said OK. So I said when? And she said she wasn't sure. So I suggested that evening. And she said that was a little inconvenient and maybe Saturday morning might be better as that was her day off. And I said I'd be there. And she said she'd be looking out for me. And I said I'd be looking out for her. And, anyway, to cut a long story short, seven am sharp Saturday morning, yours truly Gus Clover was knocking on her kitchen door, toolbox in hand and overalls on ready to tackle that mother of a washing machine.

Actually, it wasn't quite the entrance I had imagined. Lynda seemed to have forgotten I was coming and looked like she had just climbed out of bed. She was wearing her bathrobe when she finally opened the door. It was pink, the robe not the door. In fact, she didn't seem that happy to see me but I knew that she was really because for one thing there was this huge pile of dirty laundry on top of the washing machine.

So I got to work right away and found the problem. The old rubber seal in the secondary connector pipe leading to the emergency outlet, you know the piece you have to twist counter-clockwise. It had worn out. So I replaced it and she was very grateful, let me tell you. She offered me some money from an old cookie jar but I wouldn't accept it. Oh no. Not Gus Clover. I said if she really wanted to thank me she could let me take her out for dinner. I'm not slow when it comes to getting a date with a pretty girl. No sir. I'll tell you more in a minute...

Ah, now here's where another invention came about. *(He points to his left.)* Betsy Ross's house. Now she was some woman. She worked in her family's flag making and upholstery business and possibly made the first stars and stripes flag with 13 stars. *(He takes a little American flag out of his bag.)* The original design was to be a six-pointed star but she pushed for the five-pointed one, as it was easier to sew. You see, she had an inventor's mind. Half the inventions in the world have come about because of man's laziness and a desire to take shortcuts. Yes sir. Look at Skype. Probably invented by some woman who wanted to be sure that when her husband called to say he was working late at the office there wasn't a naked dancer shaking her butt behind him.

Anyway, Betsy's house was built in about 1760. Colonial style, very neat. She had three husbands you know. Busy lady. The first guy was called John Ross, probably known as J.R. He was an Anglican, she was a

Quaker so their families didn't see eye to eye and opposed their marriage. So what did the two lovers do? They got a little rowing boat and in the dead of night they rowed across the Delaware to New Jersey. There, they tied the knot. Very romantic. Unfortunately this guy Ross got blown up later in an explosion down by the river.

When I first read that I thought HELLO? Could it just possibly be that this John Ross guy was an inventor? You know, busy working on some scientific breakthrough in the lab when a couple of volatile chemicals that should never get together got together. Sadly it was nothing of the kind. He was on sentry duty guarding a munitions warehouse from the British when he fancied a smoke. He took his pipe out and a wandering spark blew him to kingdom come!

So poor little Betsy was a widow. But did she waste time? I don't think so. She met this guy Joseph Ashburn – a swashbuckler who sailed his ship the *Swallow* between Philadelphia and the West Indies trading in sugar, spices and rum. He was a small guy but very muscular. I sort of see him in my mind as Al Pacino. A kind of seafaring grocer with attitude. Anyway it wasn't long before he got captured by the British and eventually died in a prison in Plymouth, England.

So poor little Betsy was a widow again. But did she waste time? I don't think so. While Joseph was in this English prison he made friends with another privateer,

John Claypoole. And when he got out of jail he came back to Philly and gave Betsy the bad news about her husband Joseph.

And did poor little Betsy waste any time? I don't think so. She married John Claypoole.

You know all together she had seven children. *(He waves his little flag.)* I don't know when she found time to do any sewing. *(He puts the flag back into the bag.)* Lynda and I only had the one incidentally – Gus Jr. He's five now, the little darling.

Anyway I'm digressing, where was I? Washing machine, toolbox, puddles ... Oh yes! I had just asked Lynda out on a first date. Well, she looked at me, thought about it and said OK. So I said when? And she said she wasn't sure. So I suggested that evening. And she said that was a little bit inconvenient and maybe Friday might be better as that was the day she got paid. And I said don't worry about that, the meal's on me. She said that was nice of me but still insisted on Friday. So we settled on a time for me to pick her up. And she said she'd be looking out for me. And I said I'd be looking out for her. And... well... I could tell she was interested.

Women huh? Never go the direct route.

*(He points down to the ground on his right.)* Now down there in Christ Church cemetery is Benjamin Franklin's grave. Remember, I was telling you about

him earlier? He was an extraordinary man. One of the
Founding Fathers of our nation. He was a printer,
diplomat, scientist and inventor. He came up with
some great sayings. Anyone recognize any? There was
"Early to bed and early to rise, makes a man healthy,
wealthy and wise". "Where there's Marriage without
Love, there will be Love without Marriage". And my
favorite – "Three may keep a secret, if two of them are
dead".

Anyway that's where they buried him when he died on
April 17, 1790. His wife Deborah is alongside him and
their child Frankie Jr. who only lived to four before
getting smallpox, is buried beside them. It's a Philly
tradition to leave coins on his grave. The money goes
to charity. Makes sense really for the man who came
up with the saying "A penny saved is a penny earned".

*GUS takes a swig of water from a bottle.*

I always wanted to be an inventor you know. Yes sir.
Let me tell you, while all my school friends were
getting into Bruce Springsteen, stadium rock and girls,
this boy could do the fastest Rubik's cube in the
school. 'Wrist action Clover' they called me. And
while they were all out getting 'stonnned', I was in my
parents' cellar, building an automobile out of used
toilet paper rolls, old Hershey wrappers and rubber
bands. I mean who was having more fun, right?

Admittedly I made some wrong calculations. I
couldn't get the car up the wooden steps. So I thought

laterally. Inventor's brain. Turn the car into something that would be useful in a cellar. Yes sir. I invented the world's first rubber band driven, toilet roll mousetrap! I tried to sell it to a rodent control company. They didn't want to know. Their loss, my millions.

Now we're coming into Philly's 'Chinatown' area. Terrific place for a meal. Little Gus and I ate here a few weeks back and he opened a fortune cookie that read, "Help! I am being held a prisoner in a Chinese bakery." Those waiters, they like to fool around. *(He snorts with laughter.)*

Anyway I was telling you about my first date with Lynda wasn't I? I took her to *Ribs and More Ribs*, this little diner I know just off Locust Street where the steaks are perfect. Although of course Lynda didn't eat any. Not that she's a vegetarian, far from it. It's just she doesn't like to eat anything that she could wear. Anyway the meal went well, Lynda had a salad and eventually told me a little about herself; how she was lacking in self-confidence since her break up from Bruno. They'd been together for seven years and then one day he just walked out on her. She said…

*AS LYNDA:* One day he was gone. I came home and there was this note stuck on the fridge under the Homer Simpson magnet. Seems he wanted to get back to his chapter…

Chapter I said, was he into books too? Maybe he worked at the library with her.

*AS LYNDA:* No, he's a biker Gus. He loves the open road and was missing his freedom. He just wanted to get out there again and have another crack at the beer and women. Feel the wind on his bald spot...

I could see what a catch she was letting go. Anyway, she said it was over and she didn't know where he was living. She still carried a photo of him though. She showed me and all it did was get me thinking of a new way to remove facial tattoos...

Anyway, I suppose it should have sounded a little alarm bell in the brain corridors of yours truly but you know how it is. She was there looking mighty pretty and I had a thing for her so I asked if I could see her again the next evening and she said she wasn't sure. So I said when would be a good time and she suggested we meet up for a date in two weeks time on Tuesday. She said she had a lot of work up until then...

They always play hard to get don't they?

Now this building on the left is the old Reading Railroad station. The trains are long gone but there's a great Farmer's Market in there. Another great place to eat. Tasty food produced by the Amish community; I recommend it for a bite later.

Now what does the Reading Railroad remind you of? Huh? What if I was to add the Pennsylvania Railroad? Any ideas? *Monopoly*! You've got it. The board game

*Monopoly* was invented by a Philadelphian, Charles Darrow. It's true. Let me tell you, this guy is one of my heroes.

Charles Darrow was this out of work heating engineer who lived with his wife in Germantown in the 1930s. It was Depression time right? Few people had a job. So he had a lot of time on his hands – good thing for an inventor; we need space and lots of time. Anyway this Darrow guy, he used to think back to lovely vacations he'd had down by the shore in Atlantic City and he decided to make a little game about it. Now initially he marked out all the properties on the kitchen tablecloth. I don't think Mrs Charles Darrow would have been too keen; my wife Lynda would get mad if I did anything inside the house I can tell you. She insisted I was in my workshop in the cellar when I was inventing.

Anyway Darrow had this little game and he'd invite his friends to come over and play it. And it was very popular with everyone being out of a job and every-thing, y'know - playing for big money rentals and owning famous streets etc. His friends liked it and it wasn't too long before they started saying "Hey Chuck boy, any chance you could make one of those board games for me to take home and play with my kids?" And so he did. He started designing little property cards and counters and boards and sold them for four bucks each. And then someone said, "Hey Charlie, you know this *Monopoly* game should be produced commercially. Ever thought of that?" So he sent the

game to Parker Brothers and… THEY REJECTED IT!
Can you believe that? They originally turned it down
saying there were three basic flaws.

(1) The rules were too complicated and difficult to
understand.
(2) There was never an outright winner.
(3) It took far too long to play.

In fact all the things that made *Monopoly* the most
popular board game in the world. Ever!

You know my boy, Gus Jr., loves playing that game.
He always insists on being the racing car while I have
to be the old boot. He thinks that's funny does little
Gus. He's a bright kid. Make no mistake. Always
coming up with ideas. Just like me really. A chip off
the old block as they say. Not a bit like his mom. Not
that I see Lynda that much now…

On your left is the *Lord and Taylor* department store.
Originally created by John Wannamaker, the man who
invented the price tag. And of course, what do you
find in department stores everywhere? Why, the
revolving door of course. Invented by Philadelphian
Theophilus Van Kennel in 1888. I guess he didn't
know if he was coming or going when he came up
with that one. *(Snorts with laughter.)*

Anyway back to those early days dating the girl of my
dreams. I persevered with Lynda and she stopped
being so nervous when I came over. She said she was

getting comfortable with me and that I made her laugh and that's always a good sign isn't it? She and I eventually became an item. We would see each other most weekends and there was nothing I'd like better than to hear people say "Here they come again, the 'Odd Couple'" 'cos that had always been one of my favorite shows. And then one night we'd just driven back from a Phillies game and were sitting in my truck outside her house when I decided to pop the question.

*AS HIMSELF:* Honey, we've been seeing each other for a while now and you know I think the world of you...

By this stage I was trying to get the ring I'd bought for her off my little finger. I'd slipped it on so I wouldn't lose it. Now the damn thing would not budge. If it carried on I was gonna marry myself. And the Philadelphia branch of the Clovers do not do *that*.

She said to me...

*AS LYNDA:* Something wrong with your finger Gus? Rash or something?

*AS HIMSELF:* No honey, nothing like that. It's this ring I bought. It won't come off.

And she said...

*AS LYNDA:* Oh is that all. Wait till you get home and use some soap.

So I said…

*AS HIMSELF:* That's no good, I bought it for you.

And she said…

*AS LYNDA:* You bought it for me? Why do you want to give me a ring?

*AS HIMSELF:* 'Cos I love you Lynda Pickles and I want to marry you.

And she said…

*AS LYNDA:* Just as well Mr Gus Clover as I'm expecting our baby in February.

Right at that moment the ring came shooting off my finger. It went flying out through the open window straight into a hedge. I spent half the night poking around in the bushes before I found the darn thing. *(Considers this.)* If only I'd had my metal detector…

Anyway, it's funny how life turns out, don't you think?

Ah, now look skywards and you're looking at the statue of William Penn. Stuck up there on the top of our City Hall. You know, it was the one I was telling you about earlier when we were discussing my 'tilt' seat idea. Now that statue of our founder stands at 548 feet high and was designed by Alexander Milne

Calder. It's led to 'The Curse of Billy Penn'. Have you heard of that? Let me tell you…

You see, for years there was a Gentlemen's agreement that no one would ever build a building taller that the Penn statue. Then in the late 1980s they put up that office building *(He points upwards.)* 'One Liberty Place' and as you can see it's higher than Penn. In fact it's higher by 397 feet and that's when the curse started. Our sports teams haven't had a lot of luck since that skyscraper went up. Before that we weren't doing too badly. *(A beat.)* I sometimes wonder whether the curse hasn't spread over my life a little. *(He dismisses it.)* Nah, I'm not really superstitious. Us Capricorns *(or whatever star sign is appropriate on performance date)* aren't easily fooled you know.

OK, we're now driving along the Benjamin Franklin Parkway, look straight ahead of you. The Philadelphia Museum of Art designed by Julian Abele the prominent African-American architect. Isn't that an impressive building? It was down here where they had the *Live 8* concert in 2005. Some say there were a million people here that day.

I was eager to get involved. I was. I tried to get backstage a few days before; I had an idea for a laser driven 3-D revolving stage but they weren't interested. I also had a run-in with one of Bon Jovi's roadies in the parking lot. They wouldn't let me near the place after that. All I said was that they should have named their *New Jersey* album, *Pennsylvania*. Lynda liked

Bon Jovi but then she was a big rock 'n' roll fan. So
was her ex - Bruno. She said he once had the words to
Guns 'N Roses's *Sweet Child O'Mine* tattooed on the
inside of his thighs. I said who's ever gonna see them
down there?

Ah, now this is what I'm sure some of you have been
waiting for… the 'Rocky Steps'. These are the very
steps Sylvester Stallone as Rocky Balboa runs up in
the *Rocky* picture. See all those people doing just that
right now. We have a name in Philly for those people
… Tourists! *(Snorts with laughter.)*

That tree-lined road to the right of the steps is Kelly
Drive named after the Kelly family whose most
famous member was Grace Kelly the actress. I love
her films, don't you? *Rear Window*'s my favorite.
Although I could never understand why James Stewart
was always looking out the window. If I'd been holed
up in a tiny apartment with a broken leg I would have
been busy inventing things not watching people being
murdered.

*There's a screech of tires. **GUS** looks over the side of
the bus.*

Phew! Near miss there, some idiot jumping the lights.
Actually, talking of tires, do you know about Charles
Goodyear? Amazing man. He was the Philadelphian
who invented vulcanized rubber. It happened in the
1830s. Great guy. The only thing he didn't make was

any money. The company that bears his name had no
connection with him. No sir.

Not that I invent things for money. *(He considers this.)*
Not that anything I've invented has actually made any
money.

Yet.

On the right is Philly's greatest concert hall, the
Kimmel Center. They have some great concerts in
there. I love classical music. I once took Lynda in
there to see the Philadelphia Orchestra. She wasn't
impressed. She stepped outside for a smoke during
intermission and locked herself out of the building.
There was a huge commotion. The orchestra started up
again with this really moving quiet section and all we
heard was Lynda banging and yelling "Let me in! I've
paid for my seat!!".

By the way, we're driving along Broad Street. This is
where we have our 'Mummers Parade' every New
Year's Day. Great fun. There are four categories -
Comics, Fancies, String Bands, and Fancy Brigades.
Little Gus loves it. When I first took him he was just 3
years old. He sat on my shoulders and had a great
time. Unlike me. The little rascal kept pulling back on
my ears. When I got home and looked in the mirror, I
thought I'd had Botox.

Now on your left is the first hospital in the USA. How
about that? The very first. Pennsylvania Hospital was

started in 1755 by Thomas Bond and Benjamin Franklin. It's got a very special place in my heart because it's where my son Gus was born. Yes sir. 3.23 in the morning. I had to rush Lynda there in my truck. And if you look on the rooftop, you will see the sky-light that lets in the light for the original operating room. Now has that place got a tale to tell? It was opened in 1804, making it the oldest existing surgical operating room in North America. Without electricity or anesthesia, patients had to pray that they got a bright, sunny day and a skilled surgeon who was swift with the knife.

Dr. Philip Syng Physick, the father of American surgery, performed many operations here in the early 1800s. To dull the pain, the patient could choose from rum, opium or a thump on the head with a mallet!

No problems the night Gus was born though. Although Lynda was a bit difficult. She kept insisting on the rum and opium. *(Snorts with laughter.)* Only kidding...

Anyway I'm getting a bit ahead of myself chrono-logically speaking. Lynda and I got married and started settling down to the great highway of life but she got some funny cravings when she was pregnant, let me tell you. Take evenings for example. I'd come back from doing this job and we'd have something to eat. Then she'd settle down in front of the TV with her toffee-popcorn, banana custard and sardine muffins.

She was really crazy about those wildlife shows. She liked animals as long as they were in a foreign country and on TV. You know, show her an elephant or a baby kangaroo somewhere hot and she was as happy as a hippo in mud. Crazy about those animal document-aries. Probably wondering what would turn out best into shoes.

Anyway, I'd sneak down to my little workshop in the cellar and try and come up with a few ideas. That's what I love to do. Try and solve problems. Give me a conundrum and let me fix it. Whether it's something that I hadn't thought through properly like my 'solar powered night flashlight', yeah that wasn't a great success, or as complicated as my 'men's back-hair shaver' - let me have a go at it. That's when I'm happiest. Tinkering around and coming up with a result that will benefit man.

Anyway, it was a shame that Lynda didn't like real animals because it was about that time that I decided we should have a family dog. I'd always wanted one; when I was a kid we had a French poodle, 'Emman-uelle'. A bit fussy. Highly intelligent though. Didn't play with me much but bonded well with my mom who used to feed her every day with prime steak. She was crazy about her. Anyway, I was looking through the classifieds in the *Philadelphia Enquirer* one day and saw that there was this puppy place near Pottstown selling pooches. Well without telling Lynda, I drove out one afternoon and this litter came charging in with their mother and there was one who looked a little bit left out and that's always the one you go for isn't it? You know, the one all the others trample over in the rush to meet you. The mutt who gets left behind and seems to be obsessed with scratching his ear with his back paw. *(He attempts to demonstrate this.)*

That was the one for me; he was a … *(He describes breed of dog.)* I named him 'Popeye' after Popeye the sailor man; he's always been one of my favorites. I then took him home and showed him to Lynda. She wasn't impressed, she thought I'd just gone out to get some milk.

Now Lynda found Pops a bit of an inconvenience. After all puppies can be a bit of a handful with their lack of house training and generally colliding with everything not in their path but I had hopes that she would get to love him in time.

Didn't quite work out like that…

Now, we're going down South Street. Remember that song *South Street* by The Orlons? All about this area. It's where all the young people go. Y'know they've got the fashion shops, the bars, new age bookshops, tattoo parlors… Lynda's ex, Bruno, was probably a regular. I don't come down here much… It was round here where Larry Fine was born. He was one of the 'Three Stooges'. I always found them funny didn't you? Larry, Moe and Curly. Lynda couldn't stand them. Said she'd rather hold a steel golf club in a lightning storm than watch one of their routines on TV.

I guess on reflection buying Popeye just when we were about to have a little one wasn't exactly the best timing. Not that Popeye knew that we were expecting, he just carried on hurtling around the place and yapping at anything that came near our yard. Especially the cat from next door. 'Fruity' he was called and he appeared to take it upon himself to try and irritate poor little Popeye as much as possible.

One of Fruity's little tricks was to climb up a tree and stretch out as comfortably as possible on a branch. He would then start making these sort of squeaking noises *(He imitates noises.)* and that would bring an eager young Popeye, with ears pricked up, out from the house to investigate. As the squeaks got louder, Popeye would lunge down the path trying to find the location of the sound. And of course as soon as he got to the foot of the tree he would spot Fruity up on the branch. Well Popeye would do his best to try to climb the trunk but of course he couldn't get lift-off. His little paws would be scratching away trying to get a grip. He would spend hours at the base of that tree going crazy at that smug little Fruity. And then it would happen; Fruity's owner next door, Mrs Mazursky, would call for him...

*AS MRS MAZURSKY: (Makes puckering sounds with lips.)* Here Fruity? Where are you sweetheart? Mama's

got a little treat for you. Nice piece of fish. Fruity?
Fruity?

…and of course Fruity would leap off the branch and
land right on top of Popeye, flattening him. Before
Popeye could recover, Fruity was out of there. He'd
jump up on the fence and be gone. I'm telling you, that
cat had a sadistic streak.

This area is Society Hill. Very grand name but it
actually gets its name from the Society of Free Traders
in the 1700s. Isn't it a great mixture of Federal and
Georgian row houses? Very expensive. I love it around
here. If I could afford it, this is where I would live. Not
so far-fetched, I'm working on a lottery number
prediction machine as we speak.

Well… unfortunately Lynda laid down an ultimatum
about Popeye.

*AS LYNDA:* Gus, either that dog goes or I do.

Well as it happened she did. That night her waters
broke in the early hours and I had to rush her to Pennsylvania Hospital in my truck. There was a lot of
yelling and fussin'. Popeye got very excited and kept
trying to get into the truck but I had to keep telling him
no, we weren't going on a trip. His little face was so
disappointed when he was looking at us from behind
the den window, with his ears pricked up like
antennae. He must have been pretty confused with
Lynda and me running around the drive in our

pajamas. He probably thought we were going on a camping trip.

*(He points ahead.)* That's the Delaware river. Check out the Benjamin Franklin bridge; isn't it awesome? Opened in 1926, it was the longest suspension bridge in the world at the time. I love it even though it connects us to New Jersey. *(Snorts with laughter.)* Just kidding if we've got any Jerseyites on the bus.

Anyway, no one could have been a prouder father than me the night that Gus Jr. was born. It happened on February 11, which I took as a good omen seeing that it's the same date that Thomas Edison came into the world. Gus weighed in at 5 pounds which was a little on the light side. I was there at the birth, well not actually in the same room as Lynda. She was against it but I watched it through the little window in the door and filmed it on my phone.

I didn't get home until midday and then that evening I came back with Popeye to show him his new buddy; I had to sneak him in via the service elevator. I wish I hadn't done that now. There was I looking proudly at my newborn son in his glass incubator and there was Pops wreaking havoc in my wife's room by jumping up on her bed and trying to bury the digital thermometer under the sheet. And don't mention the bedpan incident! The nurses had a helluva job getting that out of Popeye's teeth. They were pulling and yelling. They blamed me too of course. But I blamed it all on the flowers in the room, Popeye probably thought he was in the park and the pan was a Frisbee!

*(GUS points.)* This area's known as Penn's Landing. It's where our founder William Penn was said to have come ashore from his ship the *Welcome* in 1682. In actual fact he landed a little further down the river in Chester but, hey, why spoil a good story with facts.

And if you look across the Delaware river you can see Camden, New Jersey on the other side. That's where RCA Victor used to manufacture gramophones and records for the first two-thirds of the twentieth century. They also made our nation's first color TV sets. How exciting is that!

Anyway, eventually we got settled into a nice little domestic routine. Gus Jr. was a lovely little boy and showed great interest in things. Very curious in how things worked. He used to wrinkle his little eyebrows in fierce concentration whenever he was trying to work out how something functioned *(GUS demonstrates this.)*. He once broke his stroller into pieces. While he was in it! Hard to believe it but he did.

It happened when Lynda took him down to the local park. At first she blamed Popeye but he was innocent. Turned out he was otherwise engaged having a vendetta with some seagulls near the wading pool. Anyway, Lynda sat down at her favorite bench and was engrossed in her Stephen King and didn't notice Gus's little fingers fiddling with the wheel nuts. Tinker,

tinker, tinker – just like his dad, tinker, tinker, tinker.
When she got up to push him towards the swings,
everything fell off and she crashed into a wire trashcan!

Of course little Gus thought it was hilarious but Lynda
didn't find it funny. In fact she came home and
accused me of deliberately teaching him how to sabot-
age his stroller. Well how could I have done that? He
was only two. But the way I saw it was that he was
thinking like an inventor. Like his dad. He was thinking laterally. He was having such a good time in the
park that he didn't want to go home. So he got to stay
by tinkering with his stroller and causing his entire
world to go crashing into a trashcan.

And of course you can be sure Popeye enjoyed the
drama. You can always tell when Pops is in a good
mood. His tail waves about like he's conducting the
Philadelphia Orchestra performing a particularly fast
version of *The Flight of the Bumblebee.*

*(He points to his left.)* Well here we are, the birthplace
of our country – Independence Hall. It was originally
the Pennsylvania State House and it's where, in the
Assembly Room, Thomas Jefferson's Declaration of
Independence was formally adopted on the 4 July
1776. Then four days later the public reading of the
Declaration took place. 8,000 people cheered their
approval. Wow! Imagine being one of the crowd on
that day. The Liberty Bell rang out on both occasions.

Of course, in 1787, the Constitution of the United States was adopted here. Afterwards Benjamin Franklin said of the sun carving on the chair where George Washington had so often sat, "I have the happiness to know that it is a rising and not a setting sun." That Ben was a profound man.

You know, sadly despite everything, Lynda and I began to drift apart. Popeye didn't help really. I had to face facts that she'd never been that fond of him. But he was my buddy; faithful and loyal. He was always there, his tail banging against the hall table, when I came in from work. Bang! Bang! Bang! Unlike Lynda who was comatose in front of the TV. No, Popeye was my little companion; he silently sat beside me while I was working on something in my cellar. I mean, don't get me wrong, Gus was also great but I couldn't really get ahead with my latest gadget whilst having to answer questions all the time on *Spider-Man*.

Popeye was my best friend. I loved that dog.

But sadly Lynda didn't.

She always insisted that I took him with me whenever I went out. Anything to get him out of the house I guess. There was one day it was snowing and I had to drive out to the King of Prussia mall to buy some chains for my truck. Popeye had jumped in the passenger's seat and was happily keeping me company and at the same time checking out the sidewalks for anything he could bark at. Now, co-incidentally, I was

working on a new kind of windshield wiper at the time
(one that wipes vertically instead of side to side) and
my attention was wandering due to this complicated
arrangement of hoses and wiper blades that kept falling off my windshield. I don't know whether it was
another dog or what but at one stage when I got out to
pick up the broken blade for the umpteenth time,
Popeye made a bolt out the door and was gone.

That was the last time I saw my dog.

I spent days looking for him. I still do. I'll never give
up. Whenever I have some time off I'm out there
searching. It's been nearly a year now but I still hold
out the hope that one day I'll find Popeye. You should
never give up, right? I must have put a sign up on
every street light in Philly. Lynda helped too; I'll say
that much. *(A beat.)* She wrote out the signs.

*(He points down to the ground on his right.)* Well
there's the Liberty Bell on show down there behind the
glass wall of The Liberty Bell Center. It was cast in
Whitechapel, London. Same people who made Big
Ben. It was originally known as the State House Bell
and it wasn't until the 1830s that it was renamed The
Liberty Bell. It's cracked a few times but there's no
finer symbol of our country. I remember the first time
I saw the Liberty Bell up close, it sort of sent a shiver
up my spine.

Now, if I'm honest, life at the Clovers wasn't that
great. Despite Popeye not being around, Lynda and I

were still drifting apart. We weren't communicating too well. Most of the time she wouldn't talk to me and on one occasion she wouldn't even look at me. That was when I was working on a new kind of matchstick and I burnt her eyebrows off! Well it was her fault for poking her nose in just when I was at my Eureka! moment. Anyway, we were breaking up. The only thing we really had in common was young Gus.

*A noisy motorbike goes by.* **GUS** *grimaces.*

Get a muffler buddy!

It was about this time that Lynda started seeing her ex, Bruno, again. It was inevitable I suppose. He was back in Philly after deciding that life as a biker wasn't all he thought it would be. The beer was messing with his prostate and the women he wanted to sleep with had other ideas. And if that wasn't enough he picked up seven speeding tickets in Nebraska and lost his license. He had to come back to Philly on the Greyhound.

Anyway, he's got himself a steady job out at the airport driving the electric courtesy cart. Yes sir if you want to get from one terminal to another, 'Tattoo Man's' your man!

Lynda moved back in with him and they've got themselves a little place in Templetown.

But at least I know where the three of them are. Yes, they took little Gus too. I immediately applied for access of course. And got it. It means every Sunday I get to take Gus out. We go to the zoo or take the ferry ride to Camden - he loves the sharks in the aquarium – he always wants me to put my hand in the water to feed them.

Sometimes he even comes out on this bus and listens to his old dad rambling on about Philly and all its secrets. I reckon he knows more about this city than I do. Certainly all the great inventors. I still miss him in the house though. Helping me make things in my cellar. I still have hopes that he may become an inventor one day but you know, I won't be all that disappointed if he doesn't. He can do whatever makes him happy. Isn't that the most important thing to pass on to your kids? Just don't end up doing something that makes you unhappy.

All I wish is that I could see more of the little rascal.

*The bus comes to a halt. We hear the hiss of the air-brakes and the engine being turned off.*

Anyway, that's the end of my tour folks. On behalf of Elvis and myself, I hope you've all had a great time and enjoyed learning a little about Philly. *(He looks anxiously over the side of the bus as if he's trying to locate someone.)* As I said earlier, today's my birthday and Lynda said she'd be bringing down little Gus to say "Happy Birthday" to me. *(He looks over the side of the bus again and this time excitedly waves at someone on the ground.)* And there's her car. You know, I've just had an idea. Would you folks like to say hello to Gus Jr.? Yeah? You would? *(His whole face lights up.)* Hang on then, I'll just pop down and bring him up. He'll get a big kick out of it. Don't go away.

*He disappears down the stairwell taking the microphone with him. We hear him talking to Lynda, off, over the loudspeakers.*

Hi? … Thanks for coming … You are joking … You are joking … Well how did that happen Lynda? … I don't believe it… Hello buddy! Hello ... Do you want to come upstairs and meet the folks? I've told them all about you … Come on …

**GUS** *reappears on the top deck. He's holding a dog in his arms.*

Ladies and Gentlemen, meet Popeye. Lynda apparently found him in some dog shelter. *(Choking back the tears.)* Wow! This has to be the best birthday ever.

*And with any luck the dog will plant a great big lick on* **Gus***'s face.*

Welcome to Philadelphia!

*Blackout.*

# Topless in Sydney
## Miles Tredinnick

Your tour guide is Amy.

The action of the play takes place on the open-top deck of a Sydney sightseeing bus a few days before Christmas.

Time: The present.

# Topless in Sydney

*The front end of an open-top Sydney sightseeing bus showing the windscreen, the two front rows of seats and the top of the stairwell. There is a bus bell button on the top of the stairwell rail. NB: The play can be staged in one of two ways; you can either use back-projection photos/videos/film of the Sydney sights or simply let **AMY**'s words paint the pictures unaided. It is entirely up to your imagination.*

*As the lights fade up we see **AMY**, a girl in her mid-twenties. She's got a great suntan as you might imagine from being a Sydney tour guide on an open-top bus. She wears a brightly coloured T-shirt and skirt and a photo ID card hangs around her neck. Her sunglasses sit on top of her head and she has a couple of festive pieces of tinsel hanging off her.*

*She is sitting across one of the seats with her feet up on the adjacent seat. She appears to be in a world of her own, staring into space. After a moment she notices her bus-load of tourists (the audience), and picks up her microphone to address them. She doesn't get to her feet for a few minutes, the effort is just too much. This is because **AMY** is suffering from the mother of all hangovers.*

### *AMY:*
G'day. How you all doing? My name's Amy and I'm your tour guide today. *(For a second she looks like she might retch but her professionalism takes over and she*

*continues.)* I'm not feeling tops to be honest. Almost
chucked a sickie this morning. Last night the company
had their Christmas party and it didn't go too well for
me. And that's an understatement. It was down on the
beach and we all rolled up on one of these buses. In
fact maybe it was this very one we're on. Anyone see
any vomit patches? Any Technicolor yawns out there?
Liquid laughs? If you spot any king prawns - that was
where I was sitting.

*She takes a swig from a water bottle. This seems to
refresh her a bit.*

I didn't mean to drink so much. *(Considers this.)*
That's a pretty dumb thing to say isn't it? As if anyone
goes out saying "Y'know tonight I'm going to deliberately drink too much and throw up like a parrot who's
eaten too much marzipan and curried egg". No, there
was a very good reason why I drunk two bottles of red,
five Bacardi Breezers and a half-bottle of Jacks.

*She pushes the bell button twice. We hear the ding-
ding and the bus starts up. It jerks off.* **AMY** *grabs a
safety rail to steady herself. From now to the end of
the play street noises can be heard where appropriate.*
**AMY** *slowly gets to her feet and attempts to put some
excitement into her tour. After all, this is her living.*

Right, here we go. We're off on a fantastic tour of the
greatest city in the world – Sydney! Yay!! *(Touches
her forehead and grimaces. Maybe a little too much
enthusiasm? She has another go.)* Sydney! ... I'm

going to show you some great places. Hope you've got
your cameras ready. If you accidentally include me in
any pix, don't be surprised if they come out a bit
fuzzy. No seriously. My head is throbbing, let me tell
you. Bang! Bang! Bang! If you plonked me in an
operating theatre, I wouldn't be the scrub nurse eyeing
up the dishy anaesthetist, I would be the heart resuscit-
ation machine! No flatlining on my watch. *(Makes a
repetitive heart-beat sound.)*

*She expertly ducks down to avoid a tree branch.*

And watch your heads! Some of these trees are very
low. In fact don't stand up. Ever. The only one who is
allowed to stand up is me and believe me it's the last
thing I want to do.

*For a second she looks like she is going to retch again
but she somehow manages not to.*

It's my own fault. I know, I know. I wasn't going to
indulge like I did. Not at the beginning anyway. You
see every Christmas our company throws a big staff
do, and to be fair to them it must have cost a bit. There
was plenty of tucker to bog into and the bar was free.
And I was a little bit nervous because they give out
these awards. It's a bit like the Oscars. In fact we call
them the Buscars. You know the kind of thing, there's
an award for the best driver and the best mechanic and
of course the best guide.

Now I've been doing this job for a couple of years and I happen to think, no I know, that I am the best tour guide in Sydney. *(Reacts to audience.)* No I am! Honest. And I knew that I was going to win that award. Now I know what you're thinking. You're thinking she doesn't seem like the best tour guide to me. Tell us about the sights? Get on with it girl will ya? Pull your finger out and point at something! But I am good. No I am. Just you wait. I often get people getting off the bus who come up to me and say "Amy, that was an extraordinary tour. When do you finish? Maybe you could carry on with your splendid commentary around some of the city's bars and clubs". It's mainly men who compliment me for some reason. I seem to be on their wavelength. Women don't seem quite as keen. It's a little strange...

*She takes another swig from her water bottle.*

That's better. Anyway, welcome to Sydney, the largest and most crazy city in all Australia. It's named after a British Home Secretary of the 1700s, Viscount Sydney. People who live here are known as 'Sydney-siders' and you'll be glad to know that I am a Sydney-sider, born and bred and proud of it. Your driver Eddie likes to think that he's a Sydneysider too but that's not really true is it Eddie? Not unless Sydney now has a suburb in Hong Kong!

*Eddie likes the name-check and gives a couple of hoots on his horn.*

We are the state capital of New South Wales and were founded in 1788 at Sydney Cove by a dude called Arthur Phillip from England. More about him later. Now I'm going to be showing you lots of our world famous sights including the Opera House and our famous 'coathanger' bridge. We won't be visiting my favourite place though – Luna Park – the best amusement park in Oz. Mind you, that's probably a good thing. I reckon if I went on their roller coaster right now I'd probably chuck up! Not that I would go on it anyway, I can't stand heights unless there's a sheet of glass between me and death.

*(She points.)* That's Darling Harbour named after some old Governor of New South Wales called Ralph Darling. It's a great place just to hang out with your mates. It's also where you can go and visit the Australian National Maritime Museum where's there a naval museum ship HMAS Vampire. Honest, that's her name. She was built out at Cockatoo Island Dockyard in the 1950s. Quite a few ships were made there and at its peak during the war there were four thousand men working on the island. I bet the local girls liked that. *(Considers this.)* The four thousand men I mean, not being stuck on Cockatoo. *(Realises she has made it worse.)* Oh shut up Amy! Reminds me of that woman who went into a bar and ordered a double entendre so the barman gave her one!! *(She laughs uproariously at this but as it hurts her head she suddenly stops.)*

Anyway, there we all were at our Christmas beach do, having a laugh and 'Gambling-Gordon', he's one of the drivers, had been taking bets about who was hot to win various awards. A few weeks before he had come up to me and said that he was certain that I was going to win 'Guide of the Year'. Gambling reckons I'm pretty tops. You see the driver can hear every word and they get a feeling of who's good and who's not. *(Calling down to her driver.)* Isn't that right Eddie?

*Eddie acknowledges her from his cab with three horn blasts.*

You like my tour, don't you?

*Eddie replies with two horn blasts.*

'Cos I'm the best, right?

*There's a pause and then we hear one weak horn blast. **AMY** reacts.*

Probably best to let him concentrate on his driving. Anyway Gambling-Gordon told me that I was going to get it. He said:

***AS GAMBLING GORDON:*** You know something, Amy. That award has your name on it. I can see the trophy now. *(Gesticulating.)* 'Amy Ellison, Guide of the Year'.

And I said:

*AS HERSELF:* Well I hope it hasn't, Gambling, 'cos my last name is Elliot. With a T.

And that seemed to cause a bit of a problem for Gambling who said he had to get off and call his mate at the engraving shop. Apparently there might be a problem…

Anyway, it made me feel good and confirmed my own feeling that I should be the winner.

We're now approaching Sydney Harbour Bridge, the 'coathanger' bridge. Just before you all get too excited we don't actually go <u>over</u> it, we go <u>under</u> it but you'll still get some great shots. The bridge was designed and built by British firm Dorman Long of Middlesbrough. I love it. It connects us to the North Shore.

There's a funny story about the day they opened it. Anybody want to hear it? Well it happened on 19th March 1932. They estimate a million people turned up to watch the opening of the bridge. It was supposed to be performed by the New South Wales Premier J.T. Lang who was going to make a fancy speech and cut the ribbon. Unfortunately he got upstaged when Captain Francis De Groot charged over on his horse and slashed the ribbon prematurely with his sword, prior to the official cutting. It was some sort of political gesture. They arrested the bounder and had to tie the ribbon back together before the ceremony could carry on. What a kerfuffle!

Did you know that in 1976 the billionth vehicle
crossed the 'coathanger'. The billionth? Wow! Mind-
blowing, eh? The first 500 million took over 33 years
and the second 500 million less than 11 years. Makes
you think doesn't it? These days up to 15,000 vehicles
can cross in just one hour. You can even take walking
tours across it. Terrifying! I've never done it. No way!
Not with my fear of heights. I get giddy just watching
Sylvester Stallone in *Cliffhanger*. *(Mimics Stallone.)*
"She was my friend, I didn't mean to let her go…"

Anyway, where was I? Oh yes, back to the beach
party. There was a bit of dancing on this floor thing
they'd rolled out over the sand and then the buffet was
unveiled. Not a bad spread if you like seafood. And I
do. I love me lobster and king prawns. Oh yes.

I was just tucking in when I caught a glimpse of
Chezza Chapman walking up. We call her 'Easter
Island Head' because she has this sort of fixed granite
expression. *(Demonstrates this.)* She's always late for
these sort of things. People think that she does it on
purpose, you know, arrive late so that people notice
her. But I don't go along with that. When you're
covered in tattoos and look like a beached whale
washed up on Bondi, people are always going to
notice you, late or not.

Most of her tattoos are of animals to be fair. She has a
giraffe on her arm, a panther on her thigh and a pair of
penguins just above her boobs. When she laughs it
looks like feeding time at the zoo. Not that I've got

anything against her. She's a very good guide in her way. Knows lots of boring historical facts and stuff. It's just that she doesn't know how to make the tour fun. Like I do. Anyway she came up to me and said:

*AS CHEZZA:* Who do you think will win the 'Guide of the Year'?

And I said:

*AS HERSELF:* I've no idea.

To which she said:

*AS CHEZZA:* A lot of people are saying it will be yours truly. One thing's for sure, it won't be you. Not after that boo-boo you made with that group of Kiwis and Coogee Beach.

Which was a bit unfair. What had happened was that I had this group from New Zealand on the bus and at the end of the tour they had been a little unappreciative in the way of tips. In fact let's not mince words here, their appreciation amounted to sweet FA. So when one of them asked me where the nearest beach to their hotel was I said it was Coogee and that if any of them wanted to swim back to New Zealand, no one would be stopping them. Apparently there was a complaint to the office or something...

Anyway, I thought her remark was a little below the belt. But that's typical of her. If she can put you down

she will. It's just her way. Makes her feel better about
herself. I'm glad I'm not like the Easter Island Head.

Now look across the water to the Sydney Opera
House. Isn't it stunning? One of the great icons of our
country. It was built by a Danish guy Jørn Utzon. He's
one of my heroes. He gained a lot of inspiration from a
trip he made through Mexico in the 1940s where he
saw the famous Mayan pyramids. They really fired his
pencil up but he admitted that the idea for the 14 shells
of the Opera House came from peeling an orange.
Clever man. Whenever I peel an orange the bloody
thing always squirts in my eye! *(She demonstrates this
in mime.)* Sadly Jørn Utzon left Australia in 1966 over
a row about suppliers and what-have-you and he never
actually saw his finished masterpiece. In fact he wasn't
even invited to the official opening by Her Majesty
Queen Elizabeth II in 1973. Very sad…

Anyway where was I? Oh yes, the Christmas party.
Well, let's backtrack a bit. As I said, a few weeks
before, Gambling-Gordon said he was sure that I was
going to win the 'Guide of the Year' award and I had
better because he stood to lose over 300 dollars if I
lost. I said "Gambling, I hope I win and I feel that I
should but if I don't it's hardly my fault. I don't want
the responsibility of you betting on the outcome." And
he said "Amy, there is a way that we can be sure of the
outcome. Be absolutely certain that I get to win all my
bets and you walk off clutching the prestigious 'Guide
of the Year' award." And I said, "how can that be
Gambling? The winners are already decided and their

names are waiting in the little gold envelopes with the easy-release adhesive backs to be read out. How could we possibly be certain of knowing that I would win?" And all he said were two words – Trevor Barncock. *(She pauses to let the name sink in.)*

*(She points.)* Now this area is known as The Rocks. Circular Quay is where Captain Arthur Phillip arrived from England in 1788 with the 11 ships of the First Fleet packed with convicts and soldiers. Originally they went to Botany Bay but that wasn't ideal so they sailed here into Sydney Cove and this is where it all began 'settlers wise'. In Arthur Phillip's first dispatch back to England he wrote "...we had the satisfaction of finding the finest harbour in the world, in which a thousand sail of the line may ride in the most perfect security..." And of course he's spot on, we do have the finest harbour in the world. As I'm sure you agree.

There were 732 convicts consisting of 543 men and 189 women, as well as 247 soldiers to guard them. 22 children too, 11 of which had been born on the voyage over from Portsmouth. *(Considers this.)* Well you have to find something to do on these long sea trips don't you?

Of course there were indigenous people already here when they arrived, the Cadigal clan of the Eora people. They'd been around for thousands of years. Unfortunately 70% of them died out in the 19th century as a result of smallpox and other viruses. They must have

been horrified when they watched that motley crew
coming ashore!

And it was no picnic, let me tell you. The convicts
were treated in a terrible way by the soldiers. Life for
our country's first settlers was brutal to say the least.
This whole area was dangerous as anything. It had
open sewers and plague-ridden rats all over the place.
It was crammed with prostitutes, thugs, vagabonds,
creeps and conmen. Not much different from today
really. *(She smiles.)* No I'm only kidding, The Rocks
is a great place to hang out.

*She takes a swig from her water bottle.*

Where was I? Creeps, conmen… Oh yes! Trevor
Barncock. He's our marketing man. He's the guy who
gets us on TV travel shows, in glossy magazines and
all over the internet. He's a funny looking guy, bald
head but colossal sideburns. Looks like a boiled egg
having a day out in a carpet warehouse. And every
Christmas the bus company give him the job of
deciding who's won the awards.

Now I've never had anything against Trevor but
apparently he was keen to redress that. It came as a
shock I can tell you.

First I didn't quite get what Gambling-Gordon was
wittering on about, I can be a bit thick like that. He
said "Trevor's got a thing for you." And I said "What
kind of thing? A letter? Something new to say on the

tour? What?" And Gambling said "No. A thing! You know." And he did that sort of chin-nod that people do when they want to convey something but for some reason can't put it into words. You know, the knowing tilt. *(She demonstrates a chin-nod.)* And that's when the penny dropped. Turned out he wanted to crack on to me!

Gambling said it was no secret amongst the drivers. "Trevor's had the hots for you since last summer, Amy".

Well… I was surprised to hear that. I had no idea, none whatsoever. Don't ask me why. Maybe it's just the way I come over. My style, you know. The way I enter a room. And Gambling quickly added "Yeah with your norks stuck out like traffic cones in front of you!"

He can be very crude can Gambling but I don't mind really 'cos he's a lovely man. He'd do anything for me. He looks after me really which is why he told me about Trevor. Well that and the bet he'd made. Anyway Gambling-Gordon had been chatting to him and certain deals had been made regarding Trevor's 'thing' for me and winning this award. More in a moment…

We're now in the CBD, the Central Business District. Lots of cars as you can see. Most of them are going around in circles looking for a space to park! *(She points.)* This is the Sydney Town Hall built in the 1880s on the site of an old cemetery. They had to move thousands of bodies from the site when they decided to build it. The steps in front of it are a popular place to meet for a date. You say "I'll meet you at the Town Hall steps." Actually, when they were renovating the building a few years ago they kept coming across corpses deep under the building. Creepy! Mind you some of the dates I've met on those steps could qualify, I can tell you...

If you look carefully at one of the carvings, you will see a lion's head with one eye closed. Some people say that it was a builder's gesture towards any women passing by. A sort of 19th century equivalent to a wolf whistle. In fact it was done by a stonemason as a back-handed compliment to his supervisor who use to shut one eye to check the stonework had been laid correctly.

Beside it is St Andrew's Cathedral built in 1868. It's the oldest cathedral in Australia. And when its twelve bells ring out on a Sunday morning, it's magical. Well let's just be grateful it's not Sunday today because my head is ringing enough as it is.

*Suddenly the bells start ringing. **AMY** is horrified.*

Oh no!!! It is Sunday isn't it? *(She covers her ears with her hands. The bells start to fade as the bus moves on.)*

Anyway back to this award shenanigans. Gambling-Gordon said it was mine provided I did certain things with Trevor Barncock. *(A look of horror.)* I said "No way, I'm not that kind of girl, Gambling." And he said that I'd got it all wrong. Trevor only wanted to take me out to dinner on a date and what was wrong with that?

Well, when he put it like that, I couldn't see the harm, particularly if it might help me win the 'Guide of the Year' award so I agreed.

Gambling said he'd ring Trevor and get him to call me. It would be strictly a dinner date, nothing heavy, just a good meal and some wine. Well, I actually started to look forward to it. I hadn't been taken out for ages.

*(She points.)* Over there is Hyde Park, 40 acres of recreational space. You see a lot of people at it in there. *(Reacts to audience.)* Jogging, I mean. It's very popular. There's all kinds of great things to see like the Archibald Fountain which honours Australia's contribution to Word War 1 in France. There's also a giant chess game you can play if that's your thing. *(She points upwards.)* And that tall building is the Sydney Tower opened in 1981. You're probably wondering how tall it is, well I can't remember exactly but let's just say it's pretty high. It's got a fabulous revolving restaurant so when Trevor announced that was where he was taking me to dinner I had mixed feelings. I've always wanted to go up there but I've a terrible head for heights. Anyway, in the end I agreed

to go. I thought if either of us dried up on the
conversation thing at least we could enjoy the view.

Well, this dinner date came up and I thought it
important not to give Trevor the wrong idea by
looking too obvious. It was important to look good
without giving out the wrong signals if you take my
meaning. I wanted him to like me and give me the
Best Guide award but no more. So I *squeezed* into my
favourite LBD and slipped on my favourite pair of
high-heels and tottered along. Trevor was already
sitting there, with his sideburns, at this table in the
revolving restaurant and he stood up when I arrived
which I thought showed good manners if nothing else.

He was dressed in a rather old fashioned way for my
liking. Had on a sort of safari suit. Looked like Roger
Moore in one of those old James Bond movies but
minus the Moneypenny quips and the hair. Anyway, I
sat down and Trevor ordered some wine and we started to chat and, to be honest, it was quite good fun. I
kept looking at this amazing view of the city which
kept changing but he kept waffling on about Jennifer
Anniston. Turned out he was a big *Friends* fan. Knew
all the episodes inside out. Which was a shame
because I didn't. So conversation was a bit limited if
you get my drift.

He said something like:

***AS TREVOR:*** Do you remember *The One with
Rachel's Going Away Party*?

And I replied…

*AS HERSELF:* Which one was that then, Trevor?

And he looked at me like I was mad and said…

*AS TREVOR:* Well, *The One with Rachel's Going Away Party*. That one. That was the name. You do know that all the episodes were called "The one where something or other", don't you Amy? I mean everyone knows that.

And I said…

*AS HERSELF:* Of course. I'm not stupid.

And he looked at me and said…

*AS TREVOR:* Which is your favourite episode then?

And I had to think really hard because to be honest I was never much of a fan of the 'Central Perk 6'. Eventually I said…

*AS HERSELF:* My favourite Trevor? My favourite was that one they never broadcast.

And one of his eyebrows shot into orbit and he said…

*AS TREVOR:* I didn't know there was an episode they didn't broadcast. What was the name of it?

And I said…

*AS HERSELF:* It was called *The One Where Rachel Gets Her Kit Off.*

Doesn't exist of course but last I heard Trevor was scouring eBay like a man possessed trying to track down a pirate bootleg.

One of my favourite things in Sydney is the El Alamein fountain over there in Fitzroy Gardens. *(She points.)* Some say it looks like a dandelion or a thistle. It was designed by New Zealander Bob Woodward and is a memorial to the soldiers who died in 1942 in two battles at El Alamein in Egypt. Isn't it beautiful? Sometime I just want to blow it like a real dandelion and make a wish…

*She pauses for a beat and reflects on this.*

We're now heading into King's Cross, known to us Sydneysiders simply as 'The Cross'. This is where people come for a good night out. Bars, restaurants, strip clubs you name it. Anything goes… What I really like here are the bronze plaques that remind us of the Cross's shady past. There's one that remembers 1930s rival brothel owners Tilly Devine and Kate Reilly, another one is for Juanita Neilson, an heiress who fought the property developers of the day. Her plaque chillingly reads 'On July 4th, 1975, Juanita attended a business meeting at the Carousel Club on this corner… and was never seen again. Believed murdered'.

There's even one that recalls Dr Jim Eakin, the so-called 'gun doc' who didn't ask his patients any awkward questions.

Oh hang on, there's something I've got to do. Eddie, pull over will you? *(She gets out her mobile phone and quickly calls a number.)* Someone said they'd give me something here. *(The bus engine switches off.* **AMY** *then speaks into her mobile.)* Hello?... It's me... I'm in The Cross now... Where are you? *(She looks down at the street in all directions trying to locate someone on the pavement.)* Where? I can't see you... *(She spots someone and waves madly.)* Yes, I can... Over here... Here!... Here!!!... HERE!!!... On top of a bloody great bus, where do you think??... Yeah, that's right... *(She waves again and then turns to the audience.)* It's my Dad, he works in a shop just off Darlinghurst Road and he's got something for me. *(She then leans over the bus and is passed up a black bin-bag containing something about a metre long. We can't see what it is.)* Cheers Dad, appreciate that... Don't worry, I won't break it... See you later...

*AMY puts the bag down on the floor under her seat.*

Sorry about that. I'll explain later. *(She speaks into the microphone again.)* Alright Eddie, let's get going.

*The bus starts up again.* **AMY** *grips a safety rail.*

Anyway, where was I? Oh yes, there we were at the top of the Tower revolving away with Trevor trying to get an eyeful down the top of my dress whenever I was looking out of the window. I have to say he did seem keen. And all the time I kept thinking what am I doing here? I had to keep saying to myself that the reason I was there was so Trevor would pick me to win the 'Guide of the Year' at the Christmas party. That was it, plain and simple. But how far did I have to go to win it? Because I wasn't going to sleep with him. *No way.*

Oh! This is Wooloomooloo. Hang on... *(She gets a Christmas party squeaker out and makes a loud noise by blowing it out.)* Always think it sounds like one of these!! WOOLOOMOOLOO ... *(She blows the squeaker again.)* One of my favourite named areas of the city. Don't you just love that name WOOLOO-MOOLOO... *(Blows the squeaker again.)* It comes from the first home built in the area, Wolloomooloo House, built by the original landowner John Palmer in 1793. There's some debate as to how he came up with the Aboriginal name. Some say that it comes from Wallamullah, meaning place of plenty, others maintain that it derives from Walamala, meaning an Aboriginal burial ground. There's even a theory that the name came from Wallabahmullah, meaning a young kang-aroo. That's the one I like. There are some fabulous apartments around here. Especially the Finger Wharf. I would love to live here. WOOLOOMOOLOO... Cool place. We Sydneysiders just call it 'The Loo'. *(Blows the squeaker again and then puts it away.)*

Anyway, Trevor and I finished the meal and I was feeling pretty good from the wine and all that. We staggered out into the street and Trevor got us a taxi. We flopped into the back seat and he told the driver to drop him off at his place in Chatswood and then take me on to my flat in Redfern. I thought it was a bit odd as they're in completely opposite directions and besides my place was much closer. But I thought maybe Trevor knew of a new route...

Then, as we neared his place, he asked would I like to pop in for a coffee? And I thought why not? I was dying to go to the dunny anyway and I was quite interested to see what kind of a place he lived in.

So I went into his apartment and had a couple of brandy nightcaps and before I knew where I was, *I was snogging him!!* That was when I located his mouth somewhere between the points of his sideburns. When I woke up in the morning I had a cracking headache and didn't have a clue where I was. And then on the bedroom bookcase I spotted a long line of *Friends* DVDs...

*(She points.)* Over there is the Royal Botanic Gardens. The oasis in the middle of our city. It was founded in 1816 so there's probably some pretty old stuff in there. It overlooks Farm Cove and was founded by Governor Macquarie. I don't know much about it to be honest but apparently it is the oldest scientific institution on Australian soil. So that's kind of impressive in an

oldest scientific institution kind of way. Looks pretty anyway.

Anyway, back to my story. That morning at Trevor's place, I noticed that his attitude to me had changed. It wasn't that he was ignoring me completely, he just wasn't sparking up any conversation over the muesli and coffee. And when he said he would give me a lift into work in his car, I expected it to be a bit further than being dropped off at the nearest bus stop on the corner. But I thought well that's because we're getting close to the Christmas party and when I win that award he doesn't want to be accused of favouritism. But it turned out that wasn't where he was coming from at all...

We're now going along Macquarie Street and you get a good view of the Parliament House built in 1816. It houses the New South Wales State Parliament and is the oldest building in Sydney. It was originally a wing of the 'Rum Hospital' which was built from the proceeds of rum duty. Those days are long gone now though. The only spirits now are the reported ghost sightings. Oh yes, the place is said to be haunted rotten. Apparently there's some old woman who can be seen sitting in a rocking chair. Many of the apparitions are seen in the old morgue which is still there but bricked up. Some people even say that a baby cries for hours but when they try and locate it, they can't! Weird or what??

Anyway, this Trevor Barncock business. When I got to work I found I had mislaid my mobile. Couldn't think where I had left it so I did that thing we all do and rang the number on a mate's phone and this guy Antonio answered it. Turned out he was a waiter at the Sydney Tower restaurant which I thought was a ridiculous coincidence as that was where I had been with Trevor the evening before.

Of course, it was then pointed out to me by Antonio that I had left it there the night before. DOH!! Silly old me. I had taken it into the ladies and left it by the basin. Some cleaning lady had found it and handed it in. Apparently she only ever kept iPhones.

Anyway, I told him I would pop in after work that day and pick it up. Antonio said he would look after it for me as if it was his own. Which it would have been if I hadn't phoned him I suppose.

*(She points.)* That lovely sandstone building on the corner of College and Park Streets is none other than the Australian Museum, which has been here since 1849. It's full of natural history and stuff. You know dinosaurs and what-have-you. Bones and stones, bugs and slugs, birds and turds. The very first custodian of the museum was a dude called William Holmes who arrived here from England. In 1831 he went on a bird collecting expedition to Moreton Bay in Queensland and accidentally shot himself with his double-barrelled fowling gun. He was actually aiming for a cockatoo at the time but missed. Apparently his final words as

witnessed by his companion Mr. Samuel Saunders
were "Oh my God, I'm dead!" The cockatoo's last
words were probably "Missed again you bastard!"

Anyway, where was I? Oh yes. My phone. So I went
back to the Sydney Tower after work that day to
retrieve it and I couldn't believe what I saw. Trevor
Barncock was in there sitting at the same table that we
had sat at the night before. I thought he must like this
place but then I saw who he was dining with. I could
only see an arm to begin with. And then I spotted this
tattooed giraffe! It was only Easter Island Head –
Chezza bloody Chapman!! *(Does her impression of
her.)* Fortunately he was so engrossed in her penguins
and she was so engrossed laughing at his jokes that
they didn't see me get my phone from Antonio and,
despite his many requests to meet up later as a reward,
slip out.

It was at that moment that the old red mist descended.
It wasn't that I was angry with the way Trevor had
used me the night before, it was that he was now doing
the same thing with her and there was a real chance
that she would win the bloody award. So I decided that
I would have to do something to make sure that never
happened. But what could I do?

Ahead of us is Central Station. It's the busiest railway
station we have and over 90,000 people use it every
day. This is where you'll find the sculpture of Donna
the Hearing Guide Dog, a 'friend and constant
companion' to one John Hogan. They were both

regulars on the trains here. Donna even made it into the Guinness World Records as the world's longest living hearing guide dog. She died at the age of 20, in 1995. Isn't that sweet?

Anyway, the first thing I thought of doing was going to the bus owners and spilling the beans on their so called marketing man Mr Trevor bloody Barncock. Tell them everything about the way that he had seduced me in order that I might win the 'Guide of the Year' award. But then the more I thought about it the more I went off the idea. I mean it was me who had agreed to stay the night at his place wasn't it? What if they said that I knew exactly what I was getting into? That I was determined to win that award at any cost? Wasn't going to make me look very good was it? And it would definitely put me out of the running for being 'Guide of the Year'.

I must admit that I did go and talk it all over with Gambling-Gordon. He was very surprised and sympathetic. That was when he stopped calling everyone on his mobile to announce that he was shortening the odds on Chezza Chapman winning. He explained that he still thought that I would win but he had to hedge his bets.

Well when he had finished hedging, I asked him what I should do? He said he couldn't really advise me as the whole situation was unprecedented. I said "Gambling, unprecedented or not, I've got to do something".

Well a couple of days later, I had a brainwave. The only way to make sure that Chezza didn't win and I did was to let it be known that she had slept with him. That way her reputation would be tarnished and she wouldn't be allowed to win the award. All I had to do was come up with a subtle way of announcing to the world that Easter Island Head was a cheat. I'll tell you my idea in a moment...

Over to our right is Haymarket where you'll find Chinatown. Fabulous place to eat. Me? I'm crazy about salt 'n' pepper squid, dumplings and crispy duck! Yum! You know, I must be feeling better to have said all that and not want to heave!! *(She smiles.)*

So... I started this dirty tricks campaign on Chezza Chapman. Something I now regret dreadfully. The first thing I did was to anonymously put up a typewritten note on the staff room notice board. I wrote "Who is going to win this year's 'Guide of the Year' award? Could it be a certain individual who has been shagging a certain egg-headed marketing man with pointed sideburns?"

Well the whole thing backfired like you wouldn't believe. The company rumour mill went well and truly into action. People started adding names underneath my words and the first 3 names up there were mine!

I was called into the office and quizzed, no 'interrogated' would be a better word, over whether there had been anything going on between me and Trevor Barncock?

I denied everything of course but the powers that be said that if anything had been going on between me and Mr Barncock that I would be instantly disqualified from the awards shortlist.

They then moved on to the next name on the list, which was Darren Topkins. He was mystified. He denied he had ever slept with Trevor and said that the man just wasn't his type. "If I wanted a man in a Safari suit, I'd go on safari, dear!" he spat at them.

The only name not on that list was Chezza bloody Chapman! So my little ruse had not worked. I had to put on my thinking cap again.

On your left is the University of Technology. Famous alumni, I like that word don't you - alumni – include none other than… Mr. Hugh Jackman. I loved him in *Les Misérables* didn't you? All that sweating and earnestness. *(Overdramatically.)* "My name is… Jean Valjean!!!" He could steal my loaf of bread any day.

I was still thinking of how to damage Chezza Chapman's chances of winning the award when I had a brainwave. Negative customer comments! Of course.

Let me explain. Our sightseeing company pay a lot of attention to our customers and what they think of our tours. So I got writing. Moan, moan, moan. Snipe,

snipe, snipe. I spent until five in the morning getting
writer's cramp saying what a crap tour guide Chezza
Chapman was.

I used six different ink colours and disguised my
handwriting by writing with my left hand, my mouth
and even my foot! (That was a shaky 83-year old ex-
Colonel from England who had retired to Adelaide and
didn't like the way Chezza had called him a whinging
pom).

I made up tourists' addresses from all over Australia,
Europe and even Easter Island. In the end I had 23
customer letters that were all united in one voice; that
Chezza Chapman was the worst tour guide in Austral-
ian history. That her Sydney tour well and truly stunk.
That she should be replaced immediately.

It was a genius ruse even if I do say so myself. My
plan was to stagger the postings over the few weeks
leading up to the awards ceremony so it didn't look
too obvious that they weren't genuine.

I stuck a stamp on each envelope and left them in a
pile next to the toaster in the kitchen. One or two a day
was what I intended sending. Unfortunately, the
master plan went tits-up when Geraldine my roomie
on her way to work at Coles popped them all into the
mail-box at once. She said she thought they were
unposted Christmas cards. I said who sends 23
Christmas cards to the same address?? She said she
hadn't read the envelopes...

The Powerhouse Museum on your left. Some amazing stuff in there including trams, trains and even a space shuttle cockpit. When I was researching the place, I was amazed to read that a lot of their collection is over at their Castle Hill Discovery Centre. Including the spare wheel of Donald Campbell's 'Bluebird' that he drove on Lake Eyre trying to break land speed records in the 1960s. What's all that about? The spare wheel?? Surely we want to see one of the wheels that actually made the attempt? Not the one that sat on the sand doing sweet FA!!!!

Well, there was hell of a kerfuffle down at the office when the postman staggered in with that sack of venom. Chezza was asked whether she knew of any vendetta towards her and she replied that no, most people enjoyed her tours and her valuable insight into Australian history.

She even gilded her lily by telling them that she had been studying at evening classes as the customers were so impressed with her knowledge and she wanted to learn more.

The outcome of all this was that goody two-shoes Miss Cheryl Chapman was more in the spotlight than ever. And with her granite expression, Easter Island Head *(Does her impression of her.)* was getting more sympathy than a widow recently widowed and about to be widowed again.

I had to put my thinking cap back on...

We're now coming up to the Sydney Fish Market
which is great if you like your fish. But who wants to
talk about fish when you're on a mission to be 'Guide
of the Year'. You're never going to believe what I did
next…

*She takes a swig from her water bottle.*

So… I considered my options. OK, I had messed up
on any pre-emptive strike to stop Chezza Chapman
getting the award. The best I could do now was to
make her cause a scene when she went up to receive it.
I therefore embarked on a mission to get her totally
maggoted at the Christmas party so that when she went
up to receive her award she'd make a speech and
totally embarrass herself.

Unfortunately it didn't go quite as I planned.

As soon as I arrived I had a few Bacardi Breezers to
get myself in the party spirit and I went looking for
her, with this bottle of goon in one hand and a bottle of
Jack Daniel's in the other. Man was I gonna get that
girl smashed. Unfortunately I couldn't find her
straightaway and I kept bumping into others who were
as determined as me to have a good time. Amazing
how much you can put away when there's a free bar,
isn't it?

By the time they announced the winners I was totally
pissed. And to my eternal shame I started heckling the
winners as they walked up to the microphone to

receive their awards. First award went to 'Mechanic of the Year' Steve Belson, well I yelled out "Bellend's got the Buscar, Bellend's got the Buscar" which at the time I thought was highly amusing.

I then added some witty repartee to Alan Wall when he won the 'Driver of the Year' by shouting out "the only wall he knows about is the one he regularly hits when he backs out of the bus depot every morning!"

Oh, how funny I thought I was at the time.

Then there was a bit of a hiccup in the proceedings. The mobile generator that was powering the PA and lights went dead and everyone was running around with screwdrivers trying to get the thing up and running again. Unfortunately this is when I decided to go and chuck a leak behind some rocks.

I say "unfortunate" because when I came back suddenly all the lights came back on and all I could see was Chezza Chapman holding the silver cup and everyone applauding.

Well I ran over, mad as hell, got hold of the mike and said "There's been a mistake, the award this year is going to me, Amy Elliot". I then grabbed the silver trophy and legged it.

I don't know why I did it. I must have been out of my mind.

I ran off into the darkness down the beach and some-where, I don't know exactly where, but somewhere I dug a hole and buried the silver trophy under the sand.

When I got back they told me that I had won the 'Guide of the Year' award and Chezza was about to present it to me.

I now have to find that cup but I don't know where it is!

*She looks around to check where they are.*

Well, here we are back at Darling Harbour where we started.

*She opens up the black bin-bag that she had earlier put on the floor under her seat and produces a metal detector and headphones. She puts the headphones around her neck.*

Now I've finished my tour I've got to go digging.

Welcome to Sydney!

*Blackout.*

**More comedies by Miles Tredinnick**

*www.MilesTredinnick.com*

# *Up Pompeii*

A comedy by Miles Tredinnick

(1 set, 6 male, 5 female)

Based on the original characters devised by Talbot
Rothwell and Sid Colin for the Frankie Howerd BBC
comedy, this hilarious romp through ancient Pompeii
brings back all the television favourites in this full-
length play. As Lurcio the slave attempts to deliver his
prologue and begin proceedings, he's quickly caught
up in the myriad of sexual liaisons in all quarters of his
master's house. Why does Ludicrus Sextus not leave
for the Senate meeting in Rome? Why does his wife
return so quickly from the country? Who will take care
of the escaped slave girl, Voluptua, and will Nausius's
love poetry improve? Whilst growing chaos ensues, an
increasing rumbling is heard in the distance – what
could that possibly be? A riot from start to finish.

*Up Pompeii* is available from
Josef Weinberger Ltd
(ISBN 978 0856763380)

## *Laugh? I Nearly Went To Miami!*

A comedy by Miles Tredinnick

(1 set, 4 male, 3 female)

*Laugh? I Nearly Went To Miami!* is a zany, fast-moving comedy of confusion. When Tom, an Elvis fanatic, and Alice his fiancée are unable, due to fog, to fly to Miami for an Elvis Convention, they arrive back at Tom's Essex flat to find they have inadvertently picked up the wrong suitcase at the airport and are now in possession of half a million dollars. Further confusion arises with the arrival of, firstly, Tom's flashy brother Barney, who is hoping to use the flat to seduce Muriel, his latest girlfriend and then Alice's eccentric Auntie with a bag containing $20,000 (a wedding present for Tom and Alice). Frankie, a thug working for the owner of the suitcase dollars adds to the chaos and it takes a real policeman, Inspector Hendy, to finally sort everything out!

*Laugh? I Nearly Went To Miami!* is available from
Samuel French Ltd
(ISBN 978 0573016332)

# *Twist*

A comedy by Miles Tredinnick

(1 set, 3 male, 3 female)

David Woods is a mild mannered accountant who sees
a sensational way of making a fortune by writing a
kiss-and-tell biography about his wife Sarah, the
nation's favourite actress from the hit TV show
*Doctors and Nurses*. He then realises that his book
will do even better if she is murdered first! Unfortunately a few obstacles get in his way...

*Twist* is a hilarious spoof of the much-loved theatrical
thriller where nobody is what they seem and nothing is
what it should be! With all the ingredients you'd
expect of a first class thriller, the cunning twists and
turns will take you on a corkscrew ride of suspense
and excitement. And just when you think you know
what's going to happen next think again, as *Twist*
catches you out one more time before the breath-
taking dénouement.

*Twist* is available from
Matador Books Ltd
(ISBN 978 1848760134)

# *It's Now or Never!*

A comedy by Miles Tredinnick

(1 set, 4 male, 3 female)

Elvis Presley fanatic Tom and his fiancée Alice arrive in Spain in preparation for their long-awaited wedding. Keith Clark, a plumber and fellow Elvis fanatic, has offered them the use of his villa outside Marbella whilst he is in London. But their arrival has been predated by a sighting by Keith of the real Elvis alive and hiding out in a nearby villa!

Unbeknownst to Alice, who is not much of an Elvis fan, Keith talks Tom into helping him kidnap Elvis to sell the story to the British tabloid press. Things go according to plan until the victim appears to die in their custody.

The ensuing confusion resulting from the attempts to hide their hysteria (and the body) from Alice while convincing The *Sunday Insider* of their conquest leads to chaos as a variety of 'Elvises' appear and disappear and identities change by the moment in this fast-paced and frenetic comedy.

*It's Now or Never!* is available from
Josef Weinberger Ltd
(ISBN 978 0856761485)

Printed in Great Britain
by Amazon